White Nationalism and Faith

Speaking of Religion

Daniel S. Brown
Series Editor

Vol. 3

The Speaking of Religion series is part of the Peter Lang
Media and Communication list.
Every volume is peer reviewed and meets
the highest quality standards for content and production.

PETER LANG
New York • Bern • Berlin
Brussels • Vienna • Oxford • Warsaw

White Nationalism and Faith

Statements and Counter-Statements
on American Identity

Camille Kaminski Lewis, Editor

PETER LANG
New York • Bern • Berlin
Brussels • Vienna • Oxford • Warsaw

Library of Congress Cataloging-in-Publication Data

Names: Lewis, Camille Kaminski, editor.
Title: White nationalism and faith: statements and counter-statements on
American identity / [edited by] Camille Kaminski Lewis.
Description: New York: Peter Lang, 2020.
Series: Speaking of religion, vol. 3
ISSN 2575-9124 (print) | ISSN 2575-9132 (online)
Includes bibliographical references.
Identifiers: LCCN 2020016967 (print) | LCCN 2020016968 (ebook)
ISBN 978-1-4331-7075-1 (hardback) | ISBN 978-1-4331-7074-4 (paperback)
ISBN 978-1-4331-7077-5 (ebook pdf) | ISBN 978-1-4331-7078-2 (epub)
ISBN 978-1-4331-7079-9 (mobi)
Subjects: LCSH: White supremacy movements—United States—History—Sources. | White
nationalism—United States—History—Sources. | White supremacy
movements—United States—Religious aspects. | White nationalism—United
States—Religious aspects. | United States—Race relations—History—
Sources. | United States—Religious life and customs.
Classification: LCC E184.A1 W3948 2020 (print) | LCC E184.A1 (ebook) |
DDC 320.56/909—dc23
LC record available at https://lccn.loc.gov/2020016967
LC ebook record available at https://lccn.loc.gov/2020016968
DOI 10.3726/b17083

Bibliographic information published by **Die Deutsche Nationalbibliothek.**
Die Deutsche Nationalbibliothek lists this publication in the "Deutsche
Nationalbibliografie"; detailed bibliographic data are available
on the Internet at http://dnb.d-nb.de/.

Table of Contents

Conclusion—Confessing America's Sin of White Nationalism

Foreword

The Speaking of Religion series advances the important principle that religious words and ideas continue to hold authority and power in an increasingly secular world. Many scholars argue that we live in a post-Christian society, that Christianity is no longer the dominate religious lens through which Americans view the culture. We concurrently hear from scholars that we live in a post-secular society. Regardless of the nomenclature, scholars of religion, sociology, and rhetoric understand that religion broadly defined has either resurged or persisted as a controlling narrative in the public sphere.

In unique ways, the current volume links speeches of the past with contemporary public concerns: immigration, labor, progressivism, urbanism, and education. In short, the public concern taken up by Professor Camille K. Lewis is White Nationalism, that conflation of significant political and religious traditions that can be traced most obviously to the years following the American Civil War.

As Professor Lewis cogently explains in her introductory chapter, White Nationalists formerly were dubbed One-hundred Percenters. It is an old concept, but with temporal nuance. It was understood that a true, one-hundred percent American in the early twentieth century meant adopting a personal identity void of any practiced connection to one's ethnicity. A person's commitment to America required disengagement from, or at least mutedness toward, one's ethnicity. Quite bluntly, it was not socially or politically acceptable to be a hyphenated American. In White Anglo Saxon Protestant America, the expectancy was that true

Americans would adapt to White Nationalism one-hundred percent of the time. Minorities were a threat to the Nation; minorities were not welcomed.

With our feet planted firmly in the twenty-first century, the most arresting feature of the nineteenth- and twentieth-century One-hundred Percent movement is its active mix of conservative politics—typically, but not exclusively Republican politics—with revivalist Evangelical Christianity. It is a stark finding to recognize the same features echoing into the current century.

At the dawn of the twenty-first century, Professor Martin J. Medhurst challenged "individual discourse communities to form their own canons through the process of rhetorical archaeology—the recovery of texts and discourses central to the self-understanding and public expression of specific groups and movements."[1] Medhurst's challenge is the basis for the *Speaking of Religion* book series, and Lewis rises to the challenge. Dr. Lewis is at her best as she unpacks the oratorical tradition of White Nationalism and its ugly sibling White supremacy. Here the reader is drawn to the unmistakable conclusion that religions, in this case specific threads of the Christian tradition, shape, influence, support, reinforce, and celebrate the link of faith with racial supremacy.

Professor Lewis is uniquely prepared to serve as pilot to this curated collection of texts, some in support of and others in opposition to One-hundred Percenters. Lewis, a scholar of rhetoric in the tradition of Kenneth Burke, has written extensively and thought deeply about racial supremacy, American nationalism, interracial animus, and the Christian faith. Dr. Lewis has authored multiple peer-reviewed articles, book chapters, and conference papers as well as a significant scholarly monograph on these topics.[2] She is a careful student of human communication who adheres to the highest ethical standards and professional expectations as she navigates the turbulent waters of race, religion, politics, and rhetoric. It is a fascinating voyage on which the reader is invited to embark.

May we listen carefully to the voices of the past as we chart our voyage into the future.

Daniel S. Brown, Jr.

Grove City, Pennsylvania

NOTES

1. Martin. J. Medhurst, "The Contemporary Study of Public Address: Renewal, Recovery, and Reconfiguration," *Rhetoric & Public Affairs* 4, no. 3 (2001): 505.
2. See for example, Camille K. Lewis, *Romancing the Difference: Kenneth Burke, Bob Jones University, and the Rhetoric of Religious Fundamentalism* (Waco, TX: Baylor University Press, 2007); Camille K. Lewis, "Fundamentalism," in *Bloomsbury Companion to Studying Christians*, eds. Stephen E. Gregg and George D. Chryssides, 2019; Camille K. Lewis, "'Remove Not the Ancient Landmarks': Making the Confederate Distortions of Religion Apparent," in *Rhetoric,*

Race, Religion, and the Charleston Shootings: Was Blind but Now I See, eds. Sean Patrick O'Rourke and Melody Lehn (Lanham, MD: Lexington Books, 2019); Camille K. Lewis, "The Ku Klux Klan and the Bible," *Encyclopedia of the Bible and Its Reception* (Berlin, Germany: De Gruyter, 2017); Camille K. Lewis, "Publish and Perish: My Fundamentalist Education from the Inside-Out," *Kenneth Burke Journal*, 2008.

Acknowledgments

I am grateful to the series editor, Daniel Brown, for his initial idea for this volume, and for Ed Appel and Clarke Rountree's early reading and guidance on the introductory chapter. All three men are gentlemen and scholars. The Furman University Humanities Development Fund granted the monies to employ Dillon Love who acquired the necessary copyright permissions and transcribed the digital copies of the artifacts for the volume. Jamie Gleeson edited an early draft. All their suggestions and contributions were helpful and welcome. The many rhetors who granted permissions were kind and supportive, and I have gained new friendships in the process.

I am also grateful to those rhetors who took umbrage at the mere suggestion that I include them in a volume on white nationalism and faith. Predictably, when I asked for permission to include artifacts that most dramatically prove the melding of white nationalism and faith, those rhetors were as pugnacious as Billy James Hargis and Carl McIntire. Their refusals themselves prove that at the intersection of politics, revivalism, and white supremacy little has changed in the United States since the Civil War—especially when a woman has the audacity to point out the obvious. I could not be more grateful to these gentlemen for their truculent evidence that when in Rome, we still need to do as the Greeks.

Camille K. Lewis

"When in Rome, Do as the Greeks!": Statements and Counter-Statements

Much of what you did in getting ready for your day this morning is habit. You did the same thing yesterday, and you will likely do the same tomorrow. You hear your alarm and clumsily pound around the nightstand looking for a way to stop it. You stagger over to the coffee pot, anxious for it to finally finish. Eventually showering, brushing, dressing, and leaving—your morning ritual is unthinking and repetitive.

The thoughtless part disturbs American rhetorician Kenneth Burke. We may need to fall into rituals for coffee and grooming, but when citizens do the same in the social and civic sphere, Burke worries about our future. When we are not aware of our own foolish customs, Burke warns, we might stumble into tragedy. He compares human beings to chickens headed for the slaughter:

> Chickens can be taught that only one specific pitch [of a ringing bell] is a food signal .... If one rings the bell next time, not to feed the chickens, but to assemble them for chopping off their heads, they come faithfully running, on the strength of the character which a ringing bell possesses for them. Chickens not so well educated would have acted more wisely. Thus it will be seen that the devices by which we arrived in the correct orientation maybe quite the same as those involved in an incorrect one.[1]

The ringing bell of our alarm triggers a similar, ritualistic behavior—what Burke calls "motion." We, like the chickens, stumble toward the next expected event without realizing a potential glitch. We have all traded urban legends about the dupe who followed Google Maps' instructions straight into an oncoming train. We wring our hands that our digital assistants are spying on us unawares—more cognizant of our own behavior than we are. We worry that the "dark mirror" we keep in our pockets might lead us to failure. We sense that we are moving with flow rather than acting with our own good sense.

As Burke continues with the metaphor, he highlights the dramatic irony we can wield as we see all the options available in the backyard coop. The chickens' "past training has caused them to misjudge their present situation. Their training has become an incapacity."[2] That unthinking and habitual motion without an awareness of the symbolic power controlling us is a "trained incapacity" that might make us run head-long toward our demise. Burke wants us to be less "fit" toward that "unfit fitness." He wants human beings not to *move* like well-trained chickens but to *act* like fully conscious human beings.[3]

To shake us from our feather-headed stupor, Burke perpetually "counter-states." William Howe Rueckert describes Burke as "always counter-stating, counter-singing against the solemnities of his system."[4] Even Burke's "stating" might irreverently become singing. He urges us to become pious toward impiety or, stated contrarily, impious toward piety. The status quo lulls us into acquiescence and rocks us toward a drowsy dependency. Any situation is familiar perhaps, Burke urges and demonstrates, but resist acting as expected. In other words, "when in Rome, do as the Greeks!"[5]

In his first volume, *Counter-Statement*, Burke explains that any idea contains its opposite as if it houses an ideological pendulum. Every principle "is matched by an opposite principle flourishing and triumphant today. Heresies and orthodoxies will always be changing places, but whatever the minority view happens to be at any given time, one must consider it as 'counter.'"[6] Every practice contains its own critique. Ideas are in dialogue, bridging gaps that we may not have known existed until the bridges were built. And alongside those bridges are other implied ways to transfer and create meaning.

In calling out "counter-statements," Burke does not want his reader to conclude that we should disagree for the sake of disagreeing. Such "negativistic" retorts are another kind of unthinking motion—like a toddler who always says "no" to whatever option is presented. Rather than being a curmudgeon simply for the social power it brings, Burke theorizes that finding an "antinomian" perspective might keep us on our toes and foreground hope for change.[7] Looking for and articulating these counter-statements are Burke's most consistent project throughout his prolific body of work.

One of Burke's famous passages imagines a scene of a living room or a lobby—a "parlor" is his term—with a loud and heated conversation in progress. The conversation is already emotional. The rivalry—the statements and their counter-statements—is obvious. Can you picture it?

> Imagine that you enter a parlor. You come late. When you arrive, others have long preceded you, and they are engaged in a heated discussion, a discussion too heated for them to pause

and tell you exactly what it is about. In fact, the discussion had already begun long before any of them got there, so that no one present is qualified to retrace for you all the steps that had gone before. You listen for a while, until you decide that you have caught the tenor of the argument; then you put in your oar. Someone answers; you answer him; another comes to your defense; another aligns himself against you, to either the embarrassment or gratification of your opponent, depending upon the quality of your ally's assistance. However, the discussion is interminable. The hour grows late, you must depart. And you do depart, with the discussion still vigorously in progress.[8]

This anthology identifies that parlor conversation at the intersection of religion, political conservatism, and white supremacy. The discussion is heated, and we do not have a lot of time to fill you in on the details. Listen here to catch the tenor of the argument, and then put in your own oar.

THE RHETORIC OF HITLER'S BATTLE: A 1938 "COUNTER-STATEMENT"

Burke most productively "puts in his oar" in his essay "The Rhetoric of Hitler's Battle." In that 1938 rhetorical criticism, Burke was doing what he imagined seven years earlier in *Counter-Statement*. He was "reaffirm[ing] democracy (government by interference, by distrust) over against Fascism (regulation by a 'benevolent' central authority)."[9]

In 1938, America was on the cusp of receiving two separately published exhaustive English translations of Adolf Hitler's *Mein Kampf*. Garth Pauley in the *KB Journal* describes the context for Burke's most famous essay.[10] Americans had a renewed interest in Hitler's ideology after the September '38 Munich Crisis in which Nazi Germany gained permission to annex Czechoslovakia. Within two weeks of the publication that winter, one translation had sold almost 30,000 copies.

The publication of Hitler's book naturally led to a surge in reviews among literary critics on the American Left. Burke was frustrated that these reviewers merely "vandalized" Hitler's Battle. Pauley frames those reviews as portraying Hitler as "delusional, insane, vulgar, and psychotic." Burke's literary cohorts were reacting in an expected "negativistic" vein. In hindsight, we could say that they were "moving," not acting. They were debunking, not engaging. Burke expands the "vandalistic" metaphor:

> The appearance of *Mein Kampf* in unexpurgated translation has called forth far too many vandalistic comments. There are other ways of burning books than on the pyre—and the favorite method of the hasty reviewer is to deprive himself and his readers by inattention. I maintain that it is thoroughly vandalistic for the reviewer to content himself with the mere inflicting of a few symbolic wounds upon this book and its author, of an intensity varying with the resources of the reviewer and the time at his disposal.[11]

To Burke his peers are no different than book-burners. Both are vandals. The term references an Enlightenment narrative that an ancient Germanic people named "Vandals" irrationally ransacked Rome. Overtime English-speakers have used that phrase to reference any destruction of property whether for sport or creativity. Keying a car or yarn-bombing a park bench—Burke puts the Hitler reviewers' product in the same category. Uselessly mowing down any existing symbol-use— whether articulated in yarn or paint or ink—is too hasty to Burke. Burke is as blunt with his peers as he is with Hitler: "If the reviewer but knocks off a few adverse attitudinizings and calls it a day, with a guaranty in advance that his article will have a favorable reception among the decent members of our population, he is contributing more to our gratification than to our enlightenment."

Mein Kampf, therefore, should not be banned from American bookstores and libraries, Burke insists. He found himself caught between the portrayal of Hitler as a deranged clown and Hitler as a never-to-be-mentioned taboo. Neither was a satisfactory response, Burke concluded. So between those two poles, Burke offers his counter-statement. He describes *Mein Kampf* as full of "Nazi magic; crude magic, but effective." Hitler, then, was neither elegant nor oafish. Instead, he was effective and dangerous. In calling their adversary unrefined and demented, Burke's peers were indulging not educating their readers.

In his critique of Hitler's Battle, Burke is careful to state that the fascist use of religious rhetoric is not organic to religion. Instead Hitler's melding is a "bastardized" faith—a perversion of a virtuous ethic.

> We must make it apparent that Hitler appeals by relying upon a bastardization of fundamentally religious patterns of thought. In this, if properly presented, there is no slight to religion. There is nothing in religion proper that requires a fascist state. There is much in religion, when misused, that does lead to a fascist state. There is a Latin proverb, *Corruptio optimi pessima*, "the corruption of the best is the worst." And it is the corrupters of religion who are a major menace to the world today, in giving the profound patterns of religious thought a crude and sinister distortion.[12]

And if Hitler could hold a great people in his wake by his rhetorical melding of hate with faith, Burke concludes, we Americans had best be careful ourselves. In the political nomenclature of the Trump presidency, we heard phrases like "Cheeto-in-Chief"—a contemporary kind of "adverse attitudinizing"—because we know that the decent members of our social media feed will be entertained and pleased. Burke would rather we were enlightened about how our own long-term choices led to this nationalistic rise to power.

Burke concludes his essay with a challenge that is eerily timely:

> Our job, then, our anti-Hitler Battle, is to find all available ways of making the Hitlerite distortions of religion apparent, in order that politicians of his kind in America be unable to perform a similar swindle. The desire for unity is genuine and admirable. The desire for

national unity, in the present state of the world, is genuine and admirable. But this unity, if attained on a deceptive basis, by emotional trickeries that shift our criticism from the accurate locus of our trouble, is no unity at all.[13]

This anthology begins in Burke's serious but antagonistic spirit. Eighty years after Burke's essay Americans find themselves sitting at our own crossroads with white nationalists or "One-Hundred Percenters"—a group twentieth-century scholars identified for their religious zealotry and knee-jerk political activism—wielding a bastardized religious rhetoric in order to justify hate and terror. How did we get here and how must we respond? Ignoring the rhetoric within the strain of One-Hundred Percenters—or what current conversations dub "white nationalists"—will vandalize our civic sphere. Knocking off a few adverse memes will only gratify ourselves. Our job, then, is to find all the available ways of making the white nationalist distortions of religion apparent, in order that politicians of this kind will be ineffective in performing their swindle.

"WHAT ARE PEOPLE DOING AND WHY ARE THEY DOING IT?": BURKE'S DRAMATISTIC METHOD

Not only does Burke challenge us to identify and counter this bastardized religious rhetoric, but also he gives us a method for understanding how it works. And through this method, we can imagine ways to counteract its power. Foundational to Burke's method is his definition of a human being not as the anthropological tool-using animal, but instead as the rhetorical "symbol-using (symbol-making, symbol-misusing) animal." Because we human beings wield symbols, we can imagine something when it is not there. We can imagine a roast beef dinner just by reading the phrase. That means, Burke deduces, that we can imagine something that is *not*. You can conclude that "whatever this is I am eating, it is not a roast beef dinner." Burke expresses this as the "inventor of the negative (or moralized by the negative)." That is, thinking of what is *not* means we can choose among things present and absent, things better or best. And yet, unfortunately our humanity and its natural state are separated because of those instruments "of our own making." Burke explains this with an example from a New York City blackout. The papers reported the next day that a "mystical terror" fell over the city because of how unnatural the darkness felt. Enlightened streets seemed normal for everyone. The darkness that pervaded a country road an hour outside NYC, however, did not seem unnatural at all.

In that separation from our natural state, we human beings are compelled to order and arrange, or as Burke says, we are "goaded by the spirit of hierarchy (or moved by the sense of order)." And that goading makes us "rotten with" our drive to reach "perfection."[14] We strive and we preen and we groom and we tinker, and that only makes us less human. This is the basic drama undergirding every use of symbols, Burke concludes. All examples of symbolic action are either perpetuating this form or countering it.

Burke frames his project as a method in the *Grammar of Motives*, where he asks "what is involved, when we say what people are doing and why they are doing it?" He identifies the "basic forms of thought" from the old "medieval questions: *quis* (agent), *quid* (act), *ubi* (scene defined as place), *quibus auxiliis* (agency), *cur* (purpose), *quo modo* (manner, 'attitude'), *quando* (scene defined temporarily)."[15] By identifying the usual issues of who, what, where, how, why, and for what ends, Burke concludes we can see the motives undergirding any action.

For instance, when a baseball player walks up to home plate with a batting helmet on his head and a bat in his hand, we can visualize an entire story about to unfold. The equipment he is wearing and the bat he is swinging are symbols—they communicate his role and his commitment to that role. The scene of the baseball diamond and field immediately clue us in to the developing events. The player is the agent, walking up to the plate. The counter agent of the pitcher from the opposing team uses hand signals to communicate with his team's catcher. The bat and ball and the cleats become the means or agency of the drama. The batter's purpose is to win for his team, for his city, or for himself. He bends his knees, leans over the plate, and angles the bat behind his ear.

What will happen next? We all know. He is not going to shoot a large orange ball into a netted hoop. He is not going to swing at a white, dimpled ball lying on a tee stuck in the ground. We know his attitude is toward hitting a baseball with that bat. Agent, act, agency, scene, purpose and attitude—these are the elements of the Burkean dramatistic hexad. Sometimes attitude—or incipient action, the next thing to happen—is cast aside for the more popular five elements of a pentad.

The motives of the baseball player and his team are not too mysterious. Symbolic action, however, might be a little more complicated. That is when rhetoricians step up to their own home plate. Imagine that you get a text from your mother which states, "We're in the car." She is describing the scene—both temporally and geographically. In describing this state of affairs, your mother is not merely communicating the fact that "we" are in a vehicle. She is communicating a whole set of expectations. She is communicating her own place as an agent—maternal, responsible for you, responsible for part of the "we" in the car. And she is communicating your agent role as well—that you, too, should be invested in this car trip wherever it may be going. She is communicating that there is an expectation of you joining the "we" and in short order (agency). She is communicating the attitude of impending and possibly urgent travel. The purpose is presumed, but you know it. She need not spell it out for you. You know that the family is going to Thanksgiving dinner, to the dentist, or maybe just to get ice cream. That entire drama is wrapped up in a single four-word text.

In a sense, the four-word text is like Aristotle's enthymeme. In Aristotle's use, according to George Kennedy, an enthymeme is more than a truncated syllogism, more than an argument with a single part missing. The enthymeme invites the listener to fill in that missing part. Stating that Socrates is a mere mortal is a mutual reference to every person's mortality and humanity. We "color in" when we see the lines.[16]

Something similar happens with symbolic action. When a parent says, "We're in the car," you fill in the expectation of speed or remind yourself of the incipient action of consuming waffle cones. You are identifying with your mother and she with you in that short sentence. Compensatory to that familial identification, Burke would want you to know, is a division. In going with your mother to Thanksgiving, you are not watching the game with your friends. "Identification is compensatory to division," Burke summarizes. One contains the other. The statement includes its own counter-statement. If a short text from a parent carries this kind of social meaning, public discourse is all that much more weighty and complex.

Burke calls this approach to rhetorical analysis, "dramatism."[17] This "method of analysis and a corresponding critique of terminology [is] designed to show that the most direct route to the study of human relations and human motives is via a methodical inquiry into cycles of clusters of terms and their functions." That is, what act is going with what agent? Or how does a particular scene compel a new act? All of Burke's dramatism centers around the "act" from which, as if it were a "god-term," all other terms "radiate." If there is an act, there must be an actor. That *actor* must be acting in some place or condition or *scene* and with some means or *agency*. If Act, Agent, Scene, and Agency work together toward some Purpose, it is not mere knee-jerk habit or motion to Burke. It is action.

The "formal interrelationships" among the terms of the pentad/hexad do overlap. Sometimes agency sounds like an end goal, and the attitude may drive the initial action. At this overlap, Burke imagines, rhetorical "alchemy" becomes possible. The five terms are also like "the fingers, which in their extremities are distinct from one another, but merge in the palm of the hand."[18] The bat and ball all work together with the player. The family members all act toward the final destination.

These pentadic/hexadic terms are not new and may not be known. But they still are doing work. Aristotle identifies them and even labels God as "pure act," a definition which resembles Church Father Thomas Aquinas' writing. In the *Nichomachean Ethics*, Aristotle concludes that even though a person "may be ignorant, then, of" his identity, action, means, location, and purpose those elements are still working together nonetheless.[19] For instance, Burke says acts and agents are usually consistent with the scene. A "brutalizing situation" will most often house "brutalized characters."[20] A baseball player acts as a baseball player on a baseball field.

Similarly, in a country that values democratic ideals, "democracy is felt to reside in us."[21]

In Burke's time a group of Southern literati associated with Vanderbilt University identified themselves as "Southern Agrarians" and sought to articulate a more politically active and intellectually savvy Lost Cause Nostalgia. Burke uses them as an example of this intimacy between agent and scene.

> When our Southern Agrarians issue a volume entitled *I'll Take My Stand* (their "stand in Dixie"), their claims as to what they *are* get defined in terms of scene, environment, context, ground. Indeed, in the title we can also see another important ambiguity of motive emerging. When taking their stand *in* Dixie, they are also taking their stand *for* Dixie. Their stand *in* Dixie would be a 'conditioning' kind of cause; but a corresponding stand *for* Dixie would be a teleological or purposive kind of cause.[22]

So if an agent acts according to his identity as an agent, Burke calls that an agent-act ratio. Similarly if an agent seeks to, as these Southern Agrarians do, express a unity between the agent and a place, that would be a scene-agent ratio.[23] How those elements contain and control each other is what Burke wants the critic to explore.

ART AS "EQUIPMENT FOR LIVING": THE STRATEGIES OF TRAGEDY AND COMEDY

Since we are "goaded to perfection" according to Burke's definition of a human being, our perfectionist drive might make us "seek to evolve terms free of ambiguity and inconsistency." Yet Burke urges us to cast that penchant aside. He wants us be "essentially enigmatic" and "comic" and "strategic." After identifying the likely tragic motives in any symbolic action, we can then imagine a counter-statement or a comic corrective.

All literature—whether proverbs or paintings or speeches—"is 'medicine.' Proverbs are designed for consolation or vengeance, for admonition or exhortation, for foretelling. Or they name typical, recurrent situations."[24] Burke lays out how even little proverbs like "Never too late to mend" are "equipment for living." They act "for promise, admonition, solace, vengeance, foretelling, instruction, charting, all for the direct bearing that such acts have upon matters of welfare." They are "*strategies* for dealing with *situations*."[25] In those strategies, they imply potential action or attitudes.[26]

Any art acts similarly. On my office wall is a portrait of young Franklin Delano Roosevelt. He glares at me while I work. That same picture in that same frame hung on my grandparents' wall next to a picture of Jesus—an economic messiah next to a spiritual one. "Roosevelt saved the house," my Grandma Kaminski would repeat.

In setting their current president alongside their universal Savior, my grandparents were acting rhetorically. We can see that drama even eighty years later. Two archetypal agents—FDR and Jesus—saved an individual scene and its residents from destruction. A larger-than-life agent focused his actions to save a particular place and people at 12600 Gallagher Avenue. Konstanty and Władysława Kaminski were creating this connection when they hung these mass-marketed portraits in the same space. They were remembering their material and spiritual salvation. They were doing rhetorical work in quilting together the divine and the political.

Burke describes the "reading of a book on attaining of success is in itself the symbolic attaining of that success."[27] In melding religion and politics on a wall in a Depression-era bungalow in Hamtramck, Michigan and in restating that "Roosevelt saved the house," my grandparents were attaining the goal of salvation. Those pictures were a "strategy for dealing with situations," as Burke would say. Two Polish immigrants and their children and grandchildren found a working-class way to "size things up" by melding the material with the spiritual. Salvation is the drama. Owning and keeping a home was as important in their minds as saving their souls.

I no longer have the picture of Jesus. I always imagined it to be the Warner Sallman *Head of Christ* painting since that was so broadly sold throughout the United States. Burke's advice continues in my head. FDR's picture would not carry the same message without its original companion. "You can't properly put" Roosevelt and Jesus "apart" (as they are currently) "until you have first put them together. First genus, then differentia. The strategy in common is the genus. The range or scale or spectrum of particularizations is the differentia."[28] That strategy in common, the genus, is salvation. That was the unified drama for my grandparents in that tiny Poletown home in metropolitan Detroit.

In sum, literature is "equipment for living" to Burke. Art—even a mass-marketed, overly-stylized picture of a president—gives us ways to find hope, warning, comfort, and information. He summarizes that "art forms like 'tragedy' or 'comedy' or 'satire' would be treated as equipment for living, that size up situations in various ways and in keeping with correspondingly various attitudes."[29] Quilting together a picture of a material savior and an immaterial Savior gave my grandparents a strategy to find "promise, admonition, solace, vengeance, foretelling, instruction, [and] charting."

Among those art forms, Burke concludes that tragedy is a primary strategy within any human endeavor, a kind of Iron Law of History. In the *Rhetoric of Religion*, he writes this poem to summarize the persistent drama:

Here are the steps
In the Iron Law of History
That welds Order and Sacrifice

Order leads to Guilt
(For who can keep commandments!)
Guilt needs Redemption
(for who would not be cleaned!)
Redemption needs Redeemer
(which is to say, a Victim!)

Order
Through Guilt
To Victimage
(hence: Cult of the Kill)…

Human beings crave order—that is, we are goaded by the spirit of hierarchy even—and will sacrifice our own in order to achieve that order. We will become rotten with our own perfection, in other words. That rottenness comes when we feel shame about not reaching the much-coveted order. We cannot even follow our own rules, and so we need redemption. Within our tragic bent, that redemption requires a person, a hero, or an archetypal victim. From hierarchical order to pervasive guilt through tumbling over the precipice of sacrifice, this is our human story. This is tragedy.

We see this strategy playing out in art. In *Romeo and Juliet*, for instance, the Capulets and the Montagues persist in an ongoing feud. Everything in the story points to a happy ending between the two teenage lovers—a consummation of their love—but their haste is their tragic flaw—a "basic sin," as Burke says, which dooms the characters to destruction. Like Romeo and Juliet, we want to ignore our tragic flaws and to think we can rise above them. That is our persistent pride— that we are bigger than our sin. Tragedies such as *Romeo and Juliet* warn us about hubris. Like Icarus, we are flying toward the sun with our waxy wings, and the very thing that raises us up will be our undoing. Our self-importance distracts us from our own limitations, and we crash to the ground.[30]

Burke wants to counter that tragedy. He wants to be the jester that runs out to Romeo before he buys the poison from the apothecary and switches it with a harmless potion. He wants to distract Romeo for a few more hours before he makes a deadly mistake—anything to forestall tragedy. In other words, Burke wants to rewrite any inevitable tragedy into a comedy. Instead of projecting all our ills on a scapegoat, Burke wants us to see that flaw in all of humanity. Romeo's haste to be with his Juliet can be juggled into teenage foolishness that averts any permanent damage just a little bit longer. Instead of Icarus flying toward the sun on wings made with of wax, Burke would tumble into a nose-dive on Icarus' launching pad, preventing his liftoff. Hubris becomes humility. Self-importance turns into a human foible. And instead of soaring, we're laughing. Burke explains:

> The progress of humane enlightenment can go no further than in picturing people not as vicious, but as mistaken. When you add that people are necessarily mistaken, that all people are exposed to situations in which they must act as fools, that every insight contains its own special kind of blindness, you complete the comic circle, returning again to the lesson of humility that underlies great tragedy.[31]

People are not evil, then, just mistaken. And we are *all* mistaken at some point. We are all fools. And so we can laugh at that shared weakness. Pride becomes stupidity. Perfection turns into hilarity. The Queen of England loses any reverent admiration when Mr. Bean enters the receiving line. The hero we would sacrifice becomes a host for *Mardi Gras*.

When Shakespeare turns to comedy, he ends the play with an engagement, a wedding, or a consummation. There is a joining together, a kind of joy over the ways separated people can cobble together happiness. In *Merchant of Venice*, for instance, all signs point to Antonio's death as Shylock demands his "pound of flesh." Portia, however, quibbles. She juggles the terms and creates a comic result. A pound of flesh is fine, she argues, but Shylock may have "no jot of blood" or else he is in violation of the law. Caught in his own quest for the letter of the law—that Iron Law of History also known as Perfection or Order—Shylock concedes, "I am content." In the end, no sacrifice is made. Antonio and Portia are reunited. And we all cheer! And hopefully, we, too, can learn to be content with imperfection in and for ourselves.

Burke likes the dramatic irony that a play foregrounds. We can see "both" sides and craft a counter-statement in mid-drama since "the audience, from its vantage point, sees the operation of errors that the characters of the play cannot see; thus seeing from two angles at once."[32] Watching the play forces us to see tragedy's own counter-statement in comedy. Perhaps comedy will distract us from a "sleeping volcano," Burke imagines, ready "to break forth and scatter destruction."[33] Dramatistically, "comedy requires the maximum of forensic complexity" and is "essentially humane."

> Humor is the opposite of the heroic. The heroic promotes acceptance by magnification, making the hero's character as agent as the situation he confronts, and fortifying the non-heroic individual vicariously, by identification with the hero; but humor reverses the process: it takes up the slack between momentousness of the situation and the feebleness of those in the situation by *dwarfing the situation*. It converts downwards, as the heroic converts upwards. Hence it does not make for so completely well-rounded a frame of acceptance as comedy, since it tends to gauge the situation falsely.[34]

Tragedy amplifies and (falsely) believes we can soar to the sun. Comedy is a counter-statement to that fatalistic fantasy. The tragedy is essentially untrue. Icarus could never fly to the sun. Speed will never unite Romeo and Juliet. The Queen of England has never been superior to Mr. Bean.

Burke explains further how literature as counter-statement can be a kind of medicine. Imagine the last time you had a fever, proof of some kind of infection your body was fighting. Your mother prescribed an allopathic—or opposite—cure. She gave you an analgesic to bring the fever down and let you rest. Her "counter-statement" was ibuprofen.

While your fever was down, you were awake enough to Google remedies for a fever. A naturalistic site suggested a homeopathic cure—replicating or intensifying the problem. If your body needs heat to fight an infection, the homeopathic argument goes, you need a warm bath. In previous centuries, Thomasonians ingested cayenne pepper to intensify the heat. The cure, they believed, was replication. Thus, counter-statements might be "like" or "unlike" statements. We might stop Icarus by all making waxy wings and all gathering at the launching pad. We all fall together and thus might see our foolishness in time. Or we may stop him by clipping his wings before he takes off for the sun.[35] Similar or opposite—either position can counter-state and, thus, thwart tragedy.

After Burke's Iron Law of History poem, he suggests that we "replace the present political stress upon men in rival international situations by a 'logological' reaffirmation of the foibles and quandaries that all men (in their role as 'symbol-using animals') have in common."[36] In other words, the secret to Burke's counter-statements is to reframe our enemies as adversaries. An evil enemy you kill; a mistaken adversary you counter, debate, resist, and oppose. Embedded in Burke is a persistently antagonistic position. The critic is always arguing, always countering, always reforming. Rather than "knock off a few adverse attitudizings" like his cohorts did with Hitler, Burke wants to speak in a full-throated resistance to Hitler's crude magic.

In sum, while Burke is warning his own crowd about passively dismissing the Aryan nationalist rhetoric steeped in religious themes, he warns us in the twenty-first century about our own homegrown white nationalism, emboldened and strengthened at the intersection with faith. We can counter-state that fascism with a more democratic drama, but first we have to take the nationalist use of religious themes seriously.

MAKING OUR DISTORTIONS OF RELIGION APPARENT: WHITE NATIONALISM AND FAITH

After the Civil War as the United States was maturing into its own world-power status, the ruling "White-Anglo-Saxon-Protestant" class began to fear European newcomers. A global economy frightened the provincial powers-that-be. Teddy Roosevelt coalesced that distrust under the epithet "hyphenated-Americans." In

1915 on Columbus Day, Roosevelt spoke to a largely Irish Catholic gathering with the Knights of Columbus in Carnegie Hall.

> There is no room in this country for hyphenated Americanism. When I refer to hyphenated Americans, I do not refer to naturalized Americans. Some of the very best Americans I have ever known were naturalized Americans, Americans born abroad. But a hyphenated American is not an American at all ... The one absolutely certain way of bringing this nation to ruin, of preventing all possibility of its continuing to be a nation at all, would be to permit it to become a tangle of squabbling nationalities, an intricate knot of German-Americans, Irish-Americans, English-Americans, French-Americans, Scandinavian-Americans or Italian-Americans, each preserving its separate nationality, each at heart feeling more sympathy with Europeans of that nationality, than with the other citizens of the American Republic ... There is no such thing as a hyphenated American who is a good American. The only man who is a good American is the man who is an American and nothing else.

Roosevelt is arguing in a sense that the dividing up of a person's identity is a mincing of loyalties. A good citizen cannot claim any ethnicity. A person is either "all in" or nothing at all. We are either a nation or "a tangle." Woodrow Wilson, too, framed the hyphen itself as a weapon. He ranted in Pueblo, Colorado in 1919 that "any man who carries a hyphen about with him carries a dagger that he is ready to plunge into the vitals of this Republic whenever he gets ready." Punctuation is a cloaked knife. Be wholly American, then, with no other noun alongside, or you are an "enemy of the Republic."[37] The drama was clear. You are either a wholly white Protestant American or you are our enemy.

The terminological stage was set then for a term to identify those who were more than just simply "American." If we can rhetorically imagine an only-American identity, we create a more-than-only-American one as well. We are goaded with the spirit of hierarchy, and so we are rotten with perfecting the most American among the Americans, a god-term of patriots.

Around the same time that powerful white male Protestant Presidents were calling Americans to a singular identity as Americans, the term "One-Hundred Percenter" merely indicated a person or a group who was fully committed to a cause such as the Red Cross, the War Chest, or the Chamber of Commerce. After the war effort diminished, however, the identity narrowed even further to categorize a particular kind of religious zealotry among the patriotic. In essence, the One-Hundred Percenter was a tireless evangelist for both God and Country—a melding of revivalism and preservationist politics. Consistently undergirding that term, however, was a sinister and persistent white supremacy. One-Hundred Percenters were aligned with the Anti-Saloon League, at this point, a coalition forged against the newly arrived immigrants. Since the un-American immigrants were brewing beer and distilling spirits, they generalized, true Americans must stop the manufacture and sale of this European poison.

For this time period, the "One-Hundred Percenter" or white nationalist was all zeal and little common sense. He whispers, imagines, and evangelizes, all with the worst dystopic fantasies in mind. Occasionally a pundit would invoke the term in an older sense to identify those same politically active zealots with more spunk than brains and more fear than research. In speaking of the Supreme Court's decision on school prayer in 1962, Catholic attorney William B. Ball blamed the One-Hundred Percenters for his being forced "to point out the bankruptcy to which legal perfectionism, one-hundred-percenter pressure tactics and a fictional history of disestablishment have now led us."[38] Ball would go on to defend those same One-Hundred Percenters—what we now call "white nationalists"—in the infamous 1983 Supreme Court case, The People of the United States vs. Bob Jones University.

For the record, however, American historian Richard Hofstadter conclusively generalizes the white nationalistic religion behind One-Hundred Percenters. In tracking the trope of anti-intellectualism throughout the American psyche, Hofstadter used the term to distinguish a fanatical conservative political agent wielding religious agency. Hofstadter blamed revivalist Billy Sunday first of all.

> One can trace in Sunday the emergence of what I would call the one-hundred per cent mentality—a mind totally committed to the full range of the dominant popular fatuities and determined that no one shall have the right to challenge them. This type of mentality is a relatively recent synthesis of fundamentalist religion and fundamentalist Americanism, very often with a heavy overlay of severe fundamentalist morality. The one-hundred per-center, who will tolerate no ambiguities, no equivocations, no reservations, and no criticism, considers his kind of connectedness and evidence of toughness and masculinity.[39]

Richard Hofstadter in 1962 sounds like Kenneth Burke in the 1930s. Note the drama at play. The hero for white nationalist religion is not thoughtful or nuanced. He—and the agent is still clearly gendered masculine—is only doggedly determined. Fundamentalist in his faith and his duty and his morality, he is … well, *right* in all three. And in his rightness, he is tough and unwavering.

Hofstadter continues with his historical summary:

> Studies of political intolerance and ethnic prejudice have shown that zealous church-going and rigid religious faith are among the most important correlates of political and ethnic animosity. It is the existence of this type of mind that sets the stage for the emergence of the One-Hundred Percenter and determines the similarity of style between the modern right-wing and fundamentalist. In fact, the conditions of the Cold War and the militant spirit bred by the constant struggle against world communism have given a fundamentalist mind a new lease on life. Like almost everything else in our world, fundamentalism itself has been considerably secularized, and this process of secularization has yielded a type of pseudo-political mentality whose way of thought is best understood against the historical background of the revivalist preacher and the camp meeting."[40]

A political revivalist or an evangelical politician—the two identities are so fused they form something completely new so that neither identity is distinguishable from the other. The One-Hundred Percenter pledges political allegiance to the Bible and responds with Constitution quotations like he is in a Sword Drill.[41]

We no longer use Hofstadter's term, but we still talk about this God-and-country zealot sometimes under the generic nomenclature, "white nationalism." The FBI is very specific in its definition. For that agency, white nationalism is a "pro-white" political movement which seeks to "promote, honor, and defend the white race" viewing "multiculturalism, diversity, and illegal immigration as direct assaults on the white race and race-mixing as akin to white genocide."[42] The South-ern Poverty Law Center defines white nationalism simply as advocating for "white supremacist or white separatist ideologies, often focusing on the alleged inferiority of nonwhites."[43] The *New York Times* highlighted political science professor Eric Kaufmann's definition of white nationalism as "the belief that national identity should be built around white ethnicity, and that white people should therefore maintain both a demographic majority and dominance of the nation's culture and public life."

Tracing arguments used on many stumps and pulpits since the Civil War reveals that appeals to white nationalism within a religious nomenclature per-sist. Whether we name these advocates "One-Hundred Percenters" or "White Nationalists," the ideology mandates similar actions for similar kinds of white male Protestants of Northern European descent. The dramas have contrary actions for every identity outside that center of white male power—for citizens of color, for non-Christians, for women, and for a wide range of sexual identities. Burke would have us counter-state these dramas. *Corruptio optimi pessima*, he cited, or "the corruption of the best is the worst." Those who have corrupted religion are a major menace, twisting the profound patterns of religious thought into a crude and sinister distortion.

OUR JOB, THEN ....

The melding of religion and nationalism is, in other words, the genus, and now we may construct the differentia. How have American rhetors since the Civil War constituted their white nationalism through religious rhetoric? And how have their contemporaries countered those statements? How can you "put in" your "oar" in the continuing conversation over the last 150 years? How can you continue Burke's public intellectual project which Rueckert describes poetically as always

> parodying the self that built the system, picking away at the overly serious dialectician, reducing the logologer to jingles, pushing the Divine comedy on over into the farce, and

returning again and again to the ironic, often comic voice of the aphorist and the small, often trivial concerns of daily life. The most serious truths can be coached into jokes. The system builder, the maker of monuments is finally to be seen as a little old man, with piercing blue eyes and white beard, standing at the base of this monument, looking up, dwarfed by the size of his own creation, realizing as he looks at it that thieves will rob its inner secret chambers, (which may be empty anyway).[44]

What is the best way for us to parody our own identities which built our current nationalistic conversation? How can we turn a sacred text into a jingle? Where do we stand at the base of our own American monuments, dwarfing us and our individual quirks so that we can create a better, more comic version of ourselves. If while we are in Rome, we should do as the Greeks, what have the Romans done and how can we be more Greek in our current time and place? Observe this collection of statements from those Hofstadter would call "One-Hundred Percenters" and their contemporaneous counter-statements. Use the same serious but comedic lens as Burke did with *Mein Kampf.* How is the symbolic action similar across the decades? How is it contrasting? What rhetorical solutions seem to be ripe with possibility for our current political scene? And as easily as some rhetors presume white rule, other religious voices contest it. Through Reconstruction, after the War to End all Wars, in the middle of a "Klanbake," through the struggle for Civil Rights, and into the Twenty-First Century—Americans have used religion to both assert and resist white rule. Each of the following sections starts with an overview and then a specific history placing the rhetor and the artifact in their cultural contexts. I include discussion questions to direct your attention at the Burkean drama at play and stir your imagination for potential counter-statements.

In framing the scholarly questions as I have, notice that I am rhetorically framing you, the reader. I see you as an actor in our current political climate, an agent who is able to make real change in an increasingly troubling world. And in the introductions of individual texts included in this book, we will focus on relevant questions drawn from this Burkean frame. The current political climate is not hopeless; you are not merely inheriting a set of problems you have to endure. Change is possible, and that change is possible with your symbolic action. We make worlds with our words after all, so let's make a better world for all of us.

NOTES

1. Kenneth Burke, *Permanence and Change: An Anatomy of Purpose* (Berkeley: University of California Press, 1984) 6–7.
2. Burke, *Permanence and Change,* 10.
3. In *Grammar of Motives,* Burke complicates this motion-action binary by referring to motion as "action-minus" or even "attitude-minus," since even "lower" order, non-symbol-using animals do

move. Kenneth Burke, *A Grammar of Motives* (Berkeley: University of California Press, 1969) 156, 237.

4. William Howe Rueckert, *Encounters with Kenneth Burke* (Urbana: University of Illinois Press, 1994) 26.

5. Kenneth Burke, *Counter-Statement* (Berkeley: University of California Press, 1931) 119.

6. Burke, *Counter-Statement*, vii.

7. Burke, *Counter-Statement*, viii.

8. Burke, *Philosophy*, 110–111.

9. Burke, *Counter-Statement*, 119.

10. Garth Pauley, "Criticism in Context: Kenneth Burke's 'The Rhetoric of Hitler's Battle,'" *KB Journal* 6, no. 1 (Fall 2009). http://www.kbjournal.org/content /criticism-context-kenneth-burkes-rhetoric-hitlers-battle.

11. Kenneth Burke, "The Rhetoric of Hitler's Battle," *The Philosophy of Literary Form* (Berkeley: University of California Press, 1973) 191.

12. Burke, "Hitler," 219.

13. Burke, "Hitler," 219–220.

14. Kenneth Burke, *Language as Symbolic Action: Essays on Life, Literature, and Method*, (Berkeley: University of California Press, 1966) 16.

15. Kenneth Burke, "Dramatism," David L. Sills, ed. *International Encyclopedia of the Social Sciences*. New York: Macmillan, 1968, 9.

16. George Kennedy, *Aristotle on Rhetoric: A Theory of Civic Discourse* (New York: Oxford University Press, 1991), p. 42.

17. Kenneth Burke, "Dramatism," 445–452.

18. Burke, *Grammar of Motives*, xxii.

19. Aristotle. *Nicomachean Ethics*. Translated by W. D. Ross. Boston: The Internet Classics Archive, 1994. http://classics.mit.edu/Aristotle/nicomachaen.html, 1111a5.

20. Burke, *Grammar*, 9.

21. Burke, *Grammar*, 17.

22. Burke, *Grammar*, 24

23. Burke, *Grammar*, 19.

24. Kenneth Burke, "Literature as Equipment for Living," *The Philosophy of Literary Form* (Berkeley: University of California Press, 1973) 293.

25. Burke, "Literature," 296.

26. Burke, "Literature," 297.

27. Burke, "Literature," 299.

28. Burke, "Literature," 302.

29. Burke, "Literature," 304.

30. Kenneth Burke, *Attitudes toward History* (Berkeley: University of California Press, 1984) 39.

31. Burke, *Attitudes*, 41.

32. Burke, *Attitudes*, 41.

33. Burke, *Attitudes*, 39.

34. Burke, *Attitudes*, 42–43.

35. Burke, *Attitudes*, 47. Note.

36. Kenneth Burke, *The Rhetoric of Religion: Studies in Logology* (Berkeley: University of California Press, 1970) 5.

37. Woodrow Wilson, "Final Address in Support of the League of Nations," September 25, 1919, Available: https://www.americanrhetoric.com/speeches/ wilsonleagueofnations.htm

38. William B. Ball, "The Forbidden Prayer," *Commonwealth*, July 27, 1962, 419–421.

39. Richard Hofstadter, *Anti-Intellectualism in American Life* (New York: Knopf Doubleday, 1963), 131.

40. Hofstadter, *Anti-Intellectualism*, 146.

41. In the twentieth-century conservative evangelicals would "drill" elementary age children on their knowledge of the books of the Bible (a literal read of Ephesians 6:17). An adult would call out a Bible reference, and the seated children would compete to find the stated passage. The child who stood up first with the correct verse won that round.

42. FBI Counterterrorism Division, "State of Domestic White Nationalist Extremist Movement in the United States," December 13, 2006, 3.

43. "White Nationalist," Southern Poverty Law Center, March 17, 2020, https://www. splcenter. org/fighting-hate/extremist-files/ideology/white-nationalist.

44. William Howe Rueckert, *Encounters with Kenneth Burke* (Urbana: University of Illinois Press, 1994) 26–27.

PART 1

Reconstructing America's Religious Rhetoric

The Civil War strained America's union, economy, confidence, and faith. In his book *Civil War as Theological Crisis*, Mark Noll identifies the theological conflict tested by the War: "Most of the country's recognized religious leaders offered a thin, simple view of God's providence and a morally juvenile view of the nation and its fate."[1] According to Noll, the anxieties of a civil war required Americans to confront and complicate their overly simplistic dependence on God. Since both the North and the South assumed God was on their own side, when one side lost, what happened to their previous views of God? The South answered with a naïve deference to God's "plan." These seemingly religious appeals in the South were, then, always secular and, as the texts in this anthology highlight, were calls to reinforce white power. In other words, the religious rhetoric masked a secular structure. The white robe of righteousness cloaked white power.

As Reconstruction progressed and the memories of the war faded, the conflict between North v. the South was not as stark as white v. Black, conservative v. progressive, and liberty v. equality. In 1880, Indiana Presbyterian William Biederwolf complained that African Americans leaving the South for Northern jobs would ruin the whole country. Emancipation, he claimed, damaged Black labor because the recently freed people of color didn't understand "freedom" "when Lincoln issued the [Emancipation] Proclamation."[2]

> They thought it forever more freed them from labor and work. They fell far short of the idea of "just as much labor, but for thyself." They missed the truth that they were endowed with citizenship under the best-looking flag and the grandest government the world has ever

known. Filled with this idea of freedom from labor the Blacks have become a lazy, indolent and consequently degraded people. In fact, in a Southern climate, it seems impossible to be otherwise. He is unwilling to work on Saturday no matter how urgent the necessity. The male is an enormous consumer of tobacco and whiskey. The female has an inordinate love for red ribbon. Both are fond of sardines.

Thus, as early as 1880 a Northern Protestant blames Lincoln for ruining America with Emancipation. As African Americans left the South for Northern manufacturing jobs, this Northern pastor sets up "Chinese labor" against "white [immigrant] labor" against "Negro labor." White nationalism and faith melded in this Northern Protestant's sermon.

The statements and counter-statements proceed from those contrasts. This section includes one pair of rhetors: Henry Grady and John Roach Straton. Henry Grady's text is the earliest one—just after Biederwolf—in which he describes the God-ordained white rule which must persist throughout the North and South for the sake of prosperity. On the cusp of World War I, however, Indiana-born Manhattan pastor John Roach Straton conflates God and Country.

NOTES

1. Mark Noll, *The Civil War as a Theological Crisis* (Chapel Hill: University of North Carolina Press, 2006) 88.
2. William Biederwolf, "The Negro Exodus," Billy Graham Center Archives, Papers of William Edward Biederwolf—Collection 195.

CHAPTER ONE

"The South and Her Problems"

HENRY GRADY

Texas State Fair, Dallas, Texas
October 26, 1887[1]

After the colossal destruction and defeat of the Civil War, no voice worked harder at promoting the myth of Southern Exceptionalism than the editor of the Atlanta Constitution, *Henry Grady. He was the primary spokesperson for the image of the "New South"—that ideology that claimed the South was a profitable resource for Northern investors.*

The year after he coined the phrase "New South" in New York City in 1896, he was down in Dallas at the Texas State Fair further expounding on the South's unique "glory and prosperity." Notice how Grady makes the "South" the primary agent in his drama. The Old South is referenced in the third-person plural—a "they" that fought to defend a place. But quickly the South is the primary actor. It stands alone and carries "two separate races" "even until the end." And in bearing that burden, the South will "work out her own salvation in the fear of God." In anthropomorphizing a region as a receiver of God's judgment and grace, what is Grady doing rhetorically?

And what role does Grady craft for the recently freedmen? Grady individuates this role—always in the singular third person. He is the "trusty" sidekick, "everywhere humble and kindly." Grady insists that the Southerner of color is not a rival, but a deferring assistant to white supremacy. White "domination" is "clear and unmistakable" for Grady, so clear that it need only be patriarchal and beneficent to its followers of color, for "the white race is the superior race. This is the declaration of no new truth." God has made it so.

Two years later at the Atlanta Exposition, African American educator Booker T. Washington would reinforce this compliant role and the divine plan of white suprem-acy. He framed African Americans as a better economic resource than "those of foreign birth and strange tongue and habits" because African Americans "will buy your surplus land, make blossom the waste places in your fields, and run your factories." In a sense, Washington is not counter-stating Grady's white supremacy but expanding and rein-forcing it.[2] How does Grady set up Washington and later conversations to judge a South which reinforces white rule as essential to economic prosperity?

Why "the South"? In an indivisible union—in a Republic against the integrity of which sword shall never be drawn or mortal hand uplifted, and in which the rich blood gathering at the common heart is sent throbbing into every part of the body politic—why is one section held separated from the rest in alien consider-ation? We can understand why this should be so in a city that has a community of local interests; or in a State still clothed in that sovereignty of which the debates of peace and the storm of war has not stripped her. But why should a number of States, stretching from Richmond to Galveston, bound together by no local inter-ests, held in no autonomy, be thus combined and drawn to a common center? That man would be absurd who declaimed in Buffalo against the wrongs of the Middle States, or who demanded in Chicago a convention for the West to consider the needs of that section.

If, then, it be provincialism that holds the South together, let us outgrow it; if it be sectionalism, let us root it out of our hearts; but if it be something deeper than these and essential to our system, let us declare it with frankness, consider it with respect, defend it with firmness, and in dignity abide its consequence. What is it that holds the Southern States—though true in thought and deed to the Union—so closely bound in sympathy today? For a century, these States champi-oned a governmental theory, but that, having triumphed in every forum, fell at last by the sword. They maintained an institution, but that, having been administered in the fullest wisdom of man, fell at last in the higher wisdom of God. They fought a war, but the prejudices of that war have died, its sympathies have broadened, and its memories are already the priceless treasure of the Republic that is cemented forever with its blood. They looked out together upon the ashes of their homes and the desolation of their fields, but out of pitiful resource they have fashioned their homes anew, and plenty rides on the springing harvests. In all the past there is nothing to draw them into essential or lasting alliance—nothing in all that heroic record that cannot be rendered unfearing from provincial hands into the keeping of American history.

But the future holds a problem in solving which the South must stand alone; in dealing with which she must come closer together than ambition or despair have driven her; and on the outcome of which her very existence depends. This problem is to carry within her body politic two separate races, and nearly equal in numbers. She must carry these races in peace, for discord means ruin. She must carry them separately, for assimilation means debasement. She must carry them in equal justice, for to this she is pledged in honor and in gratitude. She must carry them even unto the end, for in human probability she will never be quit of either.

This burden no other people bears today; on none hath it ever rested. Without precedent or companionship, the South must bear this problem—the awful responsibility of which should win the sympathy of all human kind, and the protecting watchfulness of God—alone, even unto the end. Set by this problem apart from all other peoples of the earth, and her unique position emphasized rather than relieved, as I shall show hereafter, by her material conditions, it is not only fit, but it is essential that she should hold her brotherhood unimpaired, quicken her sympathies, and in the lights or in the shadows of this surpassing problem work out her own salvation in the fear of God—but of God alone.

What shall the South do to be saved? Through what paths shall she reach the end? Through what travail, or what splendors, shall she give to the Union this section, its wealth garnered, its resources utilized, and its rehabilitation complete, and restore to the world this problem solved in such justice as the finite mind can measure, or finite hands administer? In dealing with this, I shall dwell on two points: first, the duty of the South in its relation to the race problem; second, the duty of the South in relation to its no less unique and important industrial problem.

I approach this discussion with a sense of consecration. I beg your patient and cordial sympathy. And I invoke the Almighty God, that having showered on this people His fullest riches, has put their hands to this task, that He will draw near unto us, as He drew near to troubled Israel, and lead us in the ways of honor and uprightness; even through a pillar of cloud by day, and a pillar of fire by night.

What of the Negro? This of him. I want no better friend than the black boy who was raised by my side, and who is now trudging patiently with downcast eyes and shambling figure through his lowly way in life. I want no sweeter music than the crooning of my old "mammy," now dead and gone to rest, as I heard it when she held me in her loving arms, and bending her old black face above me stole the cares from my brain, and led me smiling into sleep. I want no truer soul than that which moved the trusty slave, who for four years, while my father fought with the armies that barred his freedom, slept every night at my mother's chamber door, holding her and her children as safe as if her husband stood guard, and ready to lay down his humble life on her threshold.

History has no parallel to the faith kept by the Negro in the South during the war. Often five hundred Negroes to a single white man, and yet through these dusky throngs the women and children walked in safety, and the unprotected homes rested in peace. Unmarshaled, the black battalions moved patiently to the fields in the morning to feed the armies their idleness would have starved, and at night gathered anxiously at the big house to "hear the news from marster," though conscious that his victory made their chains enduring. Everywhere humble and kindly, the bodyguard of the helpless, the rough companion of the little ones, the observant friend, the silent sentry in his lowly cabin, the shrewd counselor, and, when the dead came home, a mourner at the open grave. A thousand torches would have disbanded every Southern army, but not one was lighted. When the master, going to a war in which slavery was involved, said to his slave, "I leave my home and loved ones in your charge," the tenderness between man and master stood disclosed. And when the slave held that charge sacred through storm and temptation, he gave new meaning to faith and loyalty. I rejoice that when freedom came to him after years of waiting, it was all the sweeter because the black hands from which the shackles fell were stainless of a single crime against the helpless ones confided to his care ....

My countrymen, right here the South must make a decision on which very much depends. Many wise men held that the white vote of the South should divide, the color line be beaten down, and the Southern States ranged on economic or moral questions as interest or belief demands. I am compelled to dissent from this view. The worst thing, in my opinion, that could happen is that the white people of the South should stand in opposing factions, with the vast mass of ignorant or purchasable Negro votes between. Consider such a status. If the Negroes were skillfully led,—and leaders would not be lacking,—it would give them the balance of power, a thing not to be considered. If their vote was not compacted, it would invite the debauching bid of factions, and drift surely to that which was the most corrupt and cunning. With the shiftless habit and irresolution of slavery days still possessing him, the Negro voter will not in this generation, adrift from war issues, become a steadfast partisan through conscience or conviction. In every community, there are colored men who redeem their race from this reproach, and who vote under reason. Perhaps in time the bulk of this race may thus adjust itself. But, through what long and monstrous periods of political debauchery this status would be reached, no tongue can tell.

The clear and unmistakable domination of the white race, dominating not through violence, not through party alliance, but through the integrity of its own vote and the largeness of its sympathy and justice through which it shall compel the support of the better classes of the colored race—that is the hope and assurance of the South. Otherwise, the Negro would be bandied from one faction to another. His credulity would be played upon, his cupidity tempted, his impulses misdirected, his passions inflamed. He would be forever in alliance with that faction which was most desperate and unscrupulous. Such a state would be worse than reconstruction, for then intelligence was banded, and its speedy triumph assured. But with intelligence and property divided, bidding and overbidding for place and patronage, irritation increasing with each conflict, the bitterness and desperation seizing every heart, political debauchery deepening as each faction staked its all in the miserable game—there would be no end to this, until our suffrage was hopelessly sullied, our people forever divided, and our most sacred rights surrendered.

One thing further should be said in perfect frankness. Up to this point, we have dealt with ignorance and corruption, but beyond this point, a deeper issue confronts us. Ignorance may struggle to enlightenment; out of corruption may come the incorruptible. God speed the day when—every true man will work and pray for its coming—the Negro must be led to know and, through sympathy, to confess that his interests and the interests of the people of the South are identical. The men who, from afar off, view this subject through the cold eye of speculation or see it distorted through partisan glasses, insist that, directly or indirectly, the negro race shall be in control of the affairs of the South. We have no fears of this; already we are attracting to us the best elements of the race, and as we proceed our alliance will broaden; external pressure but irritates and impedes. Those who would put the negro race in supremacy would work against infallible decree, for the white race can never submit to its domination, because the white race is the superior race. But the supremacy of the white race of the South must be maintained forever, and the domination of the Negro race resisted at all points and at all hazards, because the white race is the superior race. This is the declaration of no new truth. It has abided forever in the marrow of our bones, and shall run forever with the blood that feeds Anglo-Saxon hearts.

In political compliance, the South has evaded the truth, and men have drifted from their convictions. But we cannot escape this issue. It faces us wherever we turn. It is an issue that has been and will be. The races and tribes of earth are of divine origin. Behind the laws of man and the decrees of war, stands the law of God. What God hath separated let no man join together. The Indian, the Malay, the Negro, the Caucasian, these types stand as markers of God's will. Let no man tinker with the work of the Almighty. Unity of civilization, no more than unity of faith, will never be witnessed on earth. No race has risen, or will rise, above its ordained place. Here is the pivotal fact of this great matter—two races are made equal in law, and in political rights, between whom the caste of race has set an impassable gulf. This gulf is bridged by a statute, and the races are urged to cross thereon. This cannot be. The fiat of the Almighty has gone forth, and in eighteen centuries of history it is written.

We would escape this issue if we could. From the depths of its soul the South invokes from heaven "peace on earth, and good will to man." She would not, if she could, cast this race back into the condition from which it was righteously raised. She would not deny its smallest or abridge its fullest privilege. Not to lift this burden forever from her people would she do the least of these things. She must walk through the valley of the shadow, for God has so ordained. But He has ordained that she shall walk in that integrity of race that was created in His wisdom and has been perpetuated in His strength. Standing in the presence of this multitude, sobered with the responsibility of the message I deliver to the young men of the South, I declare that the truth above all others to be worn unsullied and sacred in your hearts, to be surrendered to no force, sold for no price, compromised in no necessity, but cherished and defended as the covenant of your prosperity, and the pledge of peace to your children, is that the white race must dominate for ever in the South, because it is the white race, and superior to that race by which its supremacy is threatened.

It is a race issue. Let us come to this point, and stand here. Here the air is pure and the light is clear, and here honor and peace abide. Juggling and evasion deceive not a man. Compromise and subservience have carried not a point. There is not a white man, North or South, who does not feel it stir in the gray matter of his brain and throb in his heart, not a Negro who does not feel its power. It is not a sectional issue. It speaks in Ohio and in Georgia. It speaks wherever the Anglo-Saxon touches an alien race. It has just spoken in universally approved legislation in excluding the Chinaman from our gates, not for his ignorance, vice, or corruption, but because he sought to establish an inferior race in a Republic fashioned in the wisdom and defended by the blood of a homogeneous people.

The Anglo-Saxon blood has dominated always and everywhere. It fed Alfred when he wrote the charter of English liberty; it gathered about Hampden as he stood beneath the oak; it thundered in Cromwell's veins as he fought his king; it humbled Napoleon at Waterloo; it has touched the desert and jungle with undying glory; it carried the drumbeat of England around the world and spread on every continent the gospel of liberty and of God; it established this Republic, carved it from the wilderness, conquered it from the Indians, wrested it from England, and at last, stilling its own tumult, consecrated it forever as the home of the Anglo-Saxon and the theater of his transcending achievement. Never one foot of it can be surrendered, while that blood lives in American veins and feeds American hearts, to the domination of an alien and inferior race ....

This problem is not only enduring, but it is widening. The exclusion of the Chinese is the first step in the revolution that shall save liberty and law and religion to this land, and in peace and order, not enforced on the gallows or at the bayonet's end, but proceeding from the heart of an harmonious people, shall secure in the enjoyment of the rights and the control of this Republic, the homogeneous people that established and has maintained it.

The next step will be taken when some brave statesman, looking Demagogy in the face, shall move to call to the stranger at our gates, "Who comes there?" admitting every man who seeks a home or honors our institutions and whose habit and blood will run with the native current; but excluding all who seek to plant anarchy or to establish alien men or measures on our soil; and will then demand that the standard of our citizenship be lifted and the right of acquiring our suffrage be abridged. When that day comes, and God speed its coming, the position of the South will be fully understood and everywhere approved. Until then, let us—giving the negro every right, civil and political, measured in that fullness the strong should always accord the weak, holding him in closer friendship and sympathy than he is held by those who would crucify us for his sake, realizing that on his prosperity ours depends—let us resolve that never by external pressure, or internal division, shall he establish domination, directly or indirectly, over that race that every, where has maintained its supremacy. Let this resolution be cast on the lines of equity and justice. Let it be the pledge of honest, safe, and impartial administration, and we shall command the support of the colored race itself, more dependent than any other on the bounty and protection of government. Let us be wise and patient, and we shall secure through its acquiescence what otherwise we should win through conflict and hold in insecurity.

All this is no unkindness to the Negro, but rather that he may be led in equal rights and in peace to his uttermost good. Not in sectionalism, for my heart beats true to the Union, to the glory of which your life and heart is pledged. Not in disregard of the world's opinion, for to render back this problem in the world's approval is the sum of my ambition and the height of human achievement. Not in reactionary spirit, but rather to make clear that new and grander way up which the South is marching to higher destiny, and on which I would not halt her for all the spoils that have been gathered unto parties since Catiline conspired and Caesar fought. Not in passion, my countrymen, but in reason; not in narrowness, but in breadth; that we may solve this problem in calmness and in truth, and lifting its shadows, let perpetual sunshine pour down on two races, walking together in peace and contentment. Then shall this problem have proved our blessing, and the race that threatened our ruin work our salvation as it fills our fields with the best peasantry the world has ever seen. Then the South, putting behind her all the achievements of her past—and in war and in peace they beggar eulogy—may stand upright among the nations and challenge the judgment of man and the approval of God, in having worked out in their sympathy, and in His guidance, this last and surpassing miracle of human government ....

This is the road to prosperity. It is the way to manliness and sturdiness of character. When every farmer in the South shall eat bread from his own fields and meat from his own pastures, and, disturbed by no creditor and enslaved by no debt, shall sit among his teeming gardens and orchards and vineyards and dairies and barnyards, pitching his crops in his own wisdom and growing them in independence, making cotton his clean surplus, and selling it in his own time and in his chosen market and not at a master's bidding,—getting his pay in cash and not in a receipted mortgage that discharges his debt, but does not restore his freedom,— then shall be breaking the fullness of our day ....

The South needs her sons to-day more than when she summoned them to the forum to maintain her political supremacy, more than when the bugle called them to the field to defend issues put to the arbitrament of the sword. Her old body is instinct with appeal, calling on us to come and give her fuller independence than she has ever sought in field or forum. It is ours to show that as she prospered with slaves she shall prosper still more with freemen; ours to see that from the lists she entered in poverty she shall emerge in prosperity; ours to carry the transcending traditions of the old South from which none of us can in honor or in reverence depart, unstained and unbroken into the new ....

Let every man here pledge himself in this high and ardent hour, as I pledge myself and the boy that shall follow me; every man himself and his son, hand to hand and heart to heart, that in death and earnest loyalty, in patient painstaking and care, he shall watch her interest, advance her fortune, defend her fame, and guard her honor as long as life shall last. Every man in the sound of my voice, under the deeper consecration he offers to the Union, will consecrate himself to the South. Have no ambition but to be first at her feet and last at her service,—no hope but, after a long life of devotion, to sink to sleep in her bosom, as a little child sleeps at his mother's breast and rests untroubled in the light of her smile.

NOTES

1. Henry Woodfin Grady, *The Complete Orations and Speeches of Henry W. Grady*, Edited by Edwin DuBois Shurter (New York: Hinds, Noble & Eldredge, 1910) 23–64. Public Domain.
2. Booker T. Washington, *Up from Slavery: An Autobiography* (New York: Hinds, Noble & Eldredge, 1901).

CHAPTER TWO

"Saving America That the World Might Be Saved"

JOHN ROACH STRATON

First Baptist Church, Baltimore, Maryland
July 5, 1914[1]

Historians traditionally have labeled fundamentalism as a reaction to World War I anxieties.[2] However, when the United States entered World War I on April 6, 1914, conservative Protestant ministers were already primed to meld religion with patriotism. John Roach Straton was an Indiana-born Baptist minister, best known for his decade-long stint as the pastor of Manhattan's Calvary Baptist Church on West 57th Street. At the beginning of the war, Northerner fundamentalist Straton easily melds white nationalism with his conservative faith, thus, complicating that historical conclusion.

The two kinds of people that Straton blames for ruining America's righteousness are "unevangelized" European immigrants and African Americans who do not feel "loved" in their "unequal" place in society. Compare Straton's text to Henry Grady's. Straton is a Northern preacher, and Grady is a Southern newspaper editor. For Straton, who claims to be an orthodox Protestant, religion is a tool of a white supremacist society. To whom is he referring when he says "our people"? How does his notion of "national righteousness" frame international diplomacy? How does he present those European immigrants who have entered North America? He presumes that his audience would laugh at the statement, "Let every Irishman kill a negro, and then get hung for it!" What is underlying that statement that makes it funny? Given all these distinctions he makes between his audience and those in their care, what can you deduce about his audience? Quite simply, after putting these two texts in conversation, Northern fundamentalism appears to build on Grady's New South rhetoric, enlarging it for Northern sensibilities.

Here in this rich and beautiful land, God has implanted in the ears of our people two unique and glorious ideals that have made our country notable among the nations of the earth. The first of these is *the ideal of liberty*. From the dawn of our history, our people have loved freedom. The conviction has somehow been planted deep in the American heart that all men should be free—that no human being should have another's chains clanking upon his limbs. We have believed in the worth and dignity of the individual man, and the noble ideal of liberty has shone before us like a pillar of cloud by day and a pillar of fire by night. For this ideal our fathers fought and died. It was for this that the snows of Valley Forge were stained by the bloody footprints of Washington's grenadiers. It was for this that the patriotic heart of Francis Scott Key swelled with the inspiration that gave birth to "The Star-Spangled Banner."

And side by side with this ideal of liberty has gone our other outstanding national characteristics—*the ideal of righteousness*. Our people have believed that "righteousness exalteth a nation;" that just as an individual should be honest, unselfish and pure, so also should a national exemplify these lofty virtues. However far short of this ideal we may have fallen at times in the natural weakness of men, nevertheless the conviction of national righteousness has led us, coloring all of our diplomacy and shaping our internal and external politics. We exemplified this ideal in the sixties; we renewed our loyalty to it in the war for the freedom of Cuba and in our unselfish relationship to China; and we have consistently held to it amid all the trials and temptations than have come recently in connection with the distractions of our unhappy sister Republic of Mexico to the South.

Despite Europe's criticism of our Western "crudeness" and her laughter at our "amateur diplomacy"—a diplomacy, by the way, which has won while their professional and sophisticated diplomacy has woefully failed, and has plunged the nations into war—despite these things, I say, the peoples of the earth know that ours is a righteous nation. It is this fact which leads each of them to covet our good opinion in the present crisis. Because they know that in her deepest heart America stands for the right, delegations from the warring nations of Europe are now upon our shores to plead against the inhumanity and wrongs which each of them alleges against the others.

Because, then, of the natural wealth and beauty of our home, and because of these great ideals that have led and blessed our people, it is worth our while at the present time to strive earnestly that these blessings may be safeguarded for ourselves and our children—that America may be saved, and that the principles of Jesus Christ which have produced these ideals and made us great in the past may be planted yet more deeply in the hearts of us all.

DANGER POINTS TODAY

And what, now, are the dangers that menace us today and that challenge our best efforts for the true evangelization of our country?

I suggest first of all for your thinking the danger arising from an *unassimilated foreign immigration!* Notice that I do not say merely the danger of foreign immigration. I believe in such immigration. My father came to America from the shores of old Scotland, and I believe that this one nation should be open to all who love liberty and long for the blessings which we here enjoy.

But there is a deadly danger to our ideals and institutions in the rapidity with which those of alien conceptions of religion and the State are coming, and in the slowness with which we assimilate them .... Since 1880 enough immigrants have come to us to populate Canada two and one-half times. Wipe out all the people of that great sister nation to the North of us, and from the foreigners who have domiciled themselves here within the life of one generation we could repopulate it two and one-half times over! Since 1820 nearly 23,000,000 souls have come to us from abroad, and they are coming now at the rate of over 2,000,000 a year!

Nor are we at the end of this movement. We are rather only at its beginning. When the present terrible war in Europe is over, we will have such a flood of foreign immigrants as we have never dreamed of before. They will turn away, with their tear-dimmed eyes and their broken hearts, from the ruined cities, the wrecked homes and the war-wasted fields of their native countries, and will seek happiness and peace and better opportunities in our favored land.

What will we do with them? The question is vital and insistent. What *have* we done with them in the past? Can anyone deny that we have shown but poor statesmanship in handling this problem? We have allowed the vast majority of these people to drift into our great cities, there to swell the ranks of drunkenness, vice and crime, and to offer themselves as ready tools to the hands of the corrupt and degraded politicians, who for the past generation have dominated and most of our municipal life. The greatest secret of the unspeakable political corruption in our cities is to be found precisely at this point. These people have come to us, not inherently vicious and depraved, for the most part, but we have allowed them to congest in our feverish centers of population, away from the wholesome rural environment in which they lived in Europe, and they have very naturally succumbed to the depraved and insidious influences around them.

It is a conviction of my own heart that no more foreigners should be admitted to our country unless their tickets read to some inland destination, and that none of them should be naturalized except on condition of having lived here for a term of years *in the country districts.* America's destiny is wrapped up in the life of her great cities. With the rapid increase of urban over rural population, as the cities go, so will go the nation. The greatest menace in all of our cities is the mass of unassimilated and unevangelized foreigners. They have come here with different conceptions of religion and the State from ours, and we have seen already the desecration of their "Continental Sabbath," the menace of their atheism and the red glare of their anarchism.

And what really consistent and comprehensive plans have we inaugurated or carried out to train them in the true ideals of citizenship and religion? None! In sorrow we must repeat it, none! We have played with the problem here and there, but we have never grappled with it on any large and comprehensive scale, and the time has come now when we must either Americanize and Christianize these swiftly coming millions or they will speedily paganize us!

THE RACE PROBLEM

Another danger menacing us today—a danger closely akin to the one just considered—is what has been termed the Race Problem. Here is a government whose great foundation principle is liberty and equality, and yet living under this government are two races, utterly and absolutely unequal. One race is at the summit of evolution, the very flower of human civilization. The other race is at the other end of the scale. These people are here through no choice or fault of their own. They are a lovable people, a people of much promise and of many admirable traits, but a people radically dissimilar in color and racial traits from the majority race around them. And these two unequal races, separated by the ineradicable barrier of color, are living side by side under a government whose fundamental principle is equality! What shall we do with such a situation as that! In the mere statement of the factors of this problem lies its magnitude. No civilization of the past has ever faced such a trying a menacing issue as this. What can be done with it? Certainly no summary or arbitrary solution is possible. We cannot solve it in the way suggested recently by a wag, who said, in speaking of all of America's race problems—the problem of a foreigner in the North and the negro in the South—that he had an immediate and guaranteed solution. It was this: "Let every Irishman kill a negro, and then get hung for it!"

Well, that would certainly solve it by cutting the Gordian Knot. But those of us who admire the Irish as well as those of us who love the negro, cannot agree to such a solution, though we can laugh at the humor of it.

The most necessary thing at the present time is the *creation of a right atmosphere* for the consideration of the problem. We are not yet up to a final solution. No man knows what it will be or can be. But we do know that a right spirit between the two peoples is indispensable to any final solution. The race people will never be solved by the bad negro on the one hand and the mean white man on the other. Never until we get the spirit of Jesus Christ into the hearts of both races will we have a right atmosphere for a wise consideration and a just solution of this great problem.

And may we all ask our own hearts at this point, what are we doing practically as individuals, we Christian people, toward the creation of such an atmosphere? What impression does our contact with the millions of colored servants in our homes and fields and shops make upon them? Do they feel as our servants that we are merely trying to get from them as much as possible of drudgery? Or do they feel the throb of a Christian sympathy and consideration? Are we setting before them as individual examples of prayerful and sober Christian manhood and womanhood? Or are we presenting to their gaze the picture of frivolous, selfish, pleasure-loving life? If the latter, then have we any right to expect that they shall be better than those above them?

We send our missionaries abroad to the foreign lands, and we do well—indeed as a nation we have never yet discharged even the tithe of our duty to foreign missions—but what about the foreign missionary opportunity that is presented every day to us all in the coming of millions of immigrants and in the presence of the multitudes of blacks within our doors? These are questions that in all sincerity and seriousness of soul we should take home to ourselves as we think of the mission of our country and the meaning of her glorious flag.

NOTES

1. John Roach Straton, "Saving America That the World May Be Saved," *Baltimore Sun*, July 4, 1914.
2. This interpretation began with George M. Marsden, *Fundamentalism and American Culture: The Shaping of Twentieth-Century Evangelicalism* 1870–1925 (New York: Oxford University Press, 1980), 141–152.

PART 2

Maintaining America's White Piety

When Massachusetts-born Dwight L. Moody mastered mass revivals after the Civil War, he spawned a national Sunday School movement in the North and the South. Moody's sermons centered on "muscular Christianity"—a Victorian ideal of masculine vigor and faith expressed through athleticism. Through flowery diction appropriate for postbellum audiences, Moody emphasized stamina and sacrifice over politics.[1]

Those revivalists who picked up Moody's mantle as urban crusaders, however, hardened that Protestant masculinity toward a very specific white supremacist political ideology. These are the men that Richard Hofstadter imagined when he said that the "One-Hundred Percenters" embrace "zealous church-going and rigid religious faith" saturate "political and ethnic animosity."[2] Three rhetors intersect at this moment. Two articulate religious solutions to political problems. But all three cast aspersions on their adversaries, and all three sound unusually parallel to contemporary debates. Billy Sunday is usually cited as the heir to Moody's revival reputation, but his antics on the platform resemble nothing of Moody's genteel athleticism. Sunday was an actual athlete, having played for the White Sox and the Phillies, retiring from professional baseball in 1890. The Princeton seminary faculty had little good to say about Sunday's stunts and were among his few critics. As Sunday's influence waned and he settled in at his resort on Winona Lake in Indiana, one Southern revivalist rose to prominence. Alabama-born-and-bred Bob Jones frequented Sunday's Winona Lake conferences, riding the same Northern revival circuit. Sunday and Jones both diverge from Moody's more poetic masculinity to full-throated political pugnaciousness. For them, the personal is political. That is, individual piety has civic consequences.

NOTES

1. For more on Dwight L. Moody's rhetoric, see Bruce J. Evensen, *God's Man for the Gilded Age: D. L. Moody and the Rise of Modern Mass Evangelism* (New York: Oxford University Press, 2003).
2. Richard Hofstadter, *Anti-Intellectualism in American Life* (New York: Knopf Doubleday, 1963), 146.

CHAPTER THREE

"The Theater, the Cards and the Dance"

BILLY SUNDAY

March 31, 1916
Baltimore, Maryland[1]

William Ashley "Billy" Sunday (1862–1935) started his public life in professional base-ball where he debuted with the Chicago White Sox and ended with the Phillies. He started his evangelistic career preaching mostly in Iowa and Illinois in what he called the "Kerosene district," since few towns had electricity at the time. He transported the same physical antics he made famous on the outfield to the revival stage. By 1917, Sunday was unmitigated revival tycoon, collecting close to $10,000 a week in his crusades—almost $200,000 in 2020 dollars.[2]

Sunday masked his affluence, however, with a folksy, uneducated persona—a mask often critiqued by educated Americans. For example, American poet Carl Sandburg accused Sunday of consorting with "bankers and corporation lawyers" while he was tell-ing the working class to comply with income inequities:

> *You, Billy Sunday—hell, you're only a cheap salesman, a real American bunk artist selling and selling for hard American dollars a cheap imitation of the stuff this Jesus guy said ought to be as free as air and sunlight. I tell you you're an imitation and they're all getting your number.*

> *And now Hearst has picked you up—along with the railroads and the banks and all the other big-business crooks, Hearst is boosting your game....*

> *You tell poor people living in shanties that Jesus is going to fix it up all right with them by giving them mansions in the skies after they're dead and the worms have eaten 'em.*

You tell poor people they don't need more money on payday and even if it is fierce to be out of a job, Jesus'll fix that all right—all they got to do is take Jesus the way you say.[3]

The literati were not the only ones. Labor leaders, too, were skeptical of Sunday's cooperation with the richest Americans, namely John D. Rockefeller. After a face-to-face interview with Sunday, the Labor Forum *concluded:*[4]

When facts prove that "the heaven of the rich is built on the hell of the poor," and you still permit Rockefeller to be so conspicuous at the opening of your tabernacle and to sit on your Board of Directors, you invite an ethical revolt in the minds of hundreds of thousands of working people ....

The Great Teacher took a whip of cords and lashed the money changers out of the Temple, while you have asked a representative of the most conspicuous House of Mammon in the world to sit on the platform with you, and have not accorded equal recognition to the same people whom Christ conspicuously honored when He selected fishermen and humble workers to be His spokesmen and closest associates. That goes far to nullify all the good you do.

That material difference between Sunday's cohort of the very rich and the working class gets obscured in his sermons. Sunday crafts so many binaries that the obvious one gets hidden. What dichotomies do you perceive in this 1916 Baltimore sermon on popular amusements? Sunday's usual target, booze, is only mentioned in passing. The experience of going to the theatre (live shows or motion pictures), playing with cards (poker or bridge), and learning to dance (the waltz or square dancing) he describes with lurid, vivid detail. Sunday rarely depicts the moral choices he wants his audience to make with any specifics at all. He actually tantalizes his listeners with his condemnation. He voyeuristically stands in judgment of the scantily clad, heaving bosoms while this white male minister's gaze watches and judges. Those who participate in the fun are doomed for sex work and a violent death. As Billy Sunday's bank account proves, there's big money to be made in titillating moralism that supports a powerful white nationalism.

I have a message that burns its way into your soul and into my heart. My words may be strong, and if they are you must remember they are blood red with conviction. With the cry of lost souls ringing in my ears, I cannot remain still. I must cry out.

If I can save one from going to hell, I consider myself well paid for all the vituperation and malediction that you can hurl against me because I rubbed it into your pet sins.

WOULD BE CONDEMNED IN COURT OF HUMAN DESIRES

Judged in the court of human desires I might be condemned by everybody that wants to do it, but judged in the court of human conscience and I will receive a universal verdict.

We always associate in our minds certain amusements—the theater, the cards and the dance. While some will justify one, others will condemn it. Some who play cards will seek to justify that and condemn the theater, and those who go to the theater may condemn the cards.

In my opinion, the theater is of such doubtful character that it has been relegated to the class of forbidden amusements.

You know that the theater had its beginning in the church and was intended to be the handmaid of religion. It produced so much fuss and trouble that they were compelled to drop it. Unless the theater is redeemed, it will fall by its own stinking rottenness.

Some of you may wince at some of the hot shot I am going to pour into you today, but I have no apologies to offer for anything that I may say, for the very simple reason that the devil has all kinds of engines employed in scattering seeds of evil through this old world, and if I can only pump into you enough common sense to keep you away from the theater and card playing and the dance I will have no kick coming ….

SATISFIES LUST OF WORLD

Israel Zangwill says that the playwright gets up his productions to satisfy the lust of the age and not for what good they will do the world.

Archbishop Lennan said that to go night after night to the theater is a mark of decadence.

You avoid the pest house and lepers and yet night after night you will rush to the theater to enjoy this procession of moral lepers, exposed on the stage for the plaudits of the people.

The rogue and scoundrelism and man's infidelity form the groundwork of most plays. These are paraded before the people as exhibitions of genius and fit for art. I'll shoot you so full of holes your carcass could be tanned for chair bottoms.

When the church quits pouring money into that business it will stop, and when the church of Jesus Christ stops voting for the whisky business and drinking and playing cards, and going to the theater, and stops dancing, you know those things will die.

The four rottenest things on earth have their existence because of the indulgence of the church.

Somebody says:

> After all the years of unchecked experience we will sow cards and reap gamblers; we sow the dance and reap brothels and prostitutes; we sow the saloons and reap puking drunkards, just as naturally as water runs downhill.

You listen to me. I defy anybody to contradict what I have to say about the matter.

Somebody says:

What is the matter with that preacher? Don't he believe in amusements?

DIFFERENCE BETWEEN CARDS AND CHECKERS

There is not a man in Baltimore who believes more in amusements than I do. But I believe that they should be re-creative and harmless. Nobody believes more in amusements than I.

What games do I play?

Well, I play baseball and lawn tennis, although I think that is a girl's game, and I don't like it, and I play golf and checkers and chess.

Somebody says:

What's the difference between a game of cards and a game of checkers?

Well, just as much difference as there is between Heaven and hell.

Ever since the day that cards were invented to satisfy the whims of an idiotic king they have been the tools of the gambler ....

WOMAN WILL PLAY ALL DAY FOR A WHISKBROOM

A seemingly estimable woman will tear and snort and pout through an afternoon, what for? I mean the diamond-wearing bunch; the automobile gang; the silk-gowned—that's the bunch. So she can take home a dinky cream pitcher or a whiskbroom.

There is nothing so tame as to ask a fellow to play cards for the fun of it. It doesn't make any difference whether it is penny-ante or sky limit. So we have progressive euchre, and lots of church members have cards on their tables as often as food, and they are progressing to hell ....

A woman who will play bridge whist is no better than a man who will go out and play poker, and the man who comes home with a pocket full of money won at a poker game is no worse than his wife who has been playing auction or 500 all evening for a nice bouquet that are sent to her by her church-going friends ....

You are as low down as the gambler. But, some woman says 'Mr. Sunday, I am teaching my boy to play cards so that when he grows up he won't want to play cards.'

I have heard that; but say, why don't you send your daughter to live in a brothel so that she won't want to be a prostitute when she grows up? You are a fool and a jackass to talk that way. Your argument won't hold water three minutes.

I don't care who you are, there is only one thing to do, and that is to go home and to throw away every card that you have into the furnace and get rid of the thing ....

EFFECT OF ONE'S CONDUCT IS SEEN IN OTHERS

If you don't care whether your children go to the dance and I do care you make it that much harder for me to keep my children right. But I will keep them right I have to slap my next door neighbor in the face ....

Somebody says to me:

Mr. Sunday, are you going to include the square dance?

They all look alike to me. It does not take very long to cut the corners off. There was a time in America when the stately cotillion seemed to satisfy America, but it is too slow for the hot blood of the twentieth century. They must have something that will chase hurdles through their veins. There is nothing that is so insipid for the devotee of the waltz as to dance a quadrille.

I remember years ago, over 22 years ago, my wife and I went out in Kansas to see my mother and we went out in the country to attend a Fourth of July celebration. They had spread eagle oratory and red lemonade, and the young fellows with hand-painted neckties had little blue-sashed maidens and fed them gum drops and candy hearts with reading on them. They would spend as much as 30 cents on them. They had the inevitable country dance. The upper end of the platform was on the ground and the other end on posts about as high as this platform. I stood at the corner by a barrel of ice water and Mrs. Sunday and some ladies were with me. On the platform, they were getting ready for a quadrille. A great big red-headed, freckled-face, lantern-jawed, trombone-necked fellow was the caller for the dance. (I had just as soon be chambermaid in livery stable.) He spit tobacco juice enough to drown a jackrabbit. He got into a chair and rosined his old three-stringed fiddle and said:

Salute your partners—everybody swing.

A great big strapping country fellow, big enough to pull a threshing machine, had a fat voluptuous country girl for a partner and he threw his arms around her and lifted her feet right off the floor and she shot her heels right at my head.

I said to my wife:

"Well, Nellie; they all look alike to me. The round and square dances are the same."...

If there were nothing but card players and dancers in the church it would stink and rot out.

The lowest down rascal in any community is a dancing Methodist.

I am not going to give any more of these deliverances to the churches, but I have more. This is enough to show you that anybody in the church that does these things is at variance with the church.

GET A DIVORCE FROM CHURCH TO DANCE WITH THE DEVIL

I do not know of anything that is wrong for a church member to do that is not equally wrong for those that are not church members to do. The only difference between the church member and the worldling is that the church members had promised to refrain and you have not.

I tell you what I would do if I were in the church, and I was bound to dance and play cards—I would leave the church. I would not stay in it. Get out and then you can be referred to as an ex-church member who got divorced from Jesus Christ so that you could dance with the devil ....

The dancing Christian never was a soul winner. The dance is simply a hugging match set to music. The dance is a sexual love feast. This crusade against the dance is for everybody, not merely for the preacher or the old man or woman who couldn't dance if they wanted to, but for everybody interested in morals, whether in the church or out of the church.

I am preaching a sermon that Jew or Gentile, Catholic or Protestant, infidel or Christian, if he wants better morals he can stand on my side ....

WOULD NOT BE TOLERATED IN ANY OTHER PLACE

Supposing that you go to a dance tonight and then tomorrow you go around to some man's house when he is not there, that you might effectively impress upon his wife the dance and its necessary attendance and requisites. You intend to give instruction and you go in perfect innocence. You assume the same position and attitude with your arms about her that you would take on the ballroom floor. The husband comes in the back door and sees you there with your arms about his wife, and bang! Bang! Goes the revolver, and you fall dead. You could not find a jury of married men on God's dirt that would convict him. I would have just one vote—and it would be: Go home.

You cannot get around the circumstances. Is not that true about the position? Any man knows it is. It does not do any harm to keep away and it may ruin your daughter to let her go.

Do you go with your wife to the dance? You don't dance and she is a fiend. You stand there and watch man after man as he claims her hand and puts his name on her list. Perhaps that fellow was her lover and you won her hand—and you stand there and watch your wife folded in his long, voluptuous, sensual embrace, their bodies swaying one against the other, their limbs twinning and entwining, her head resting on his breast, they breathe the vitiated air beneath the glittering candelabra and the spell of the music, and you stand there and tell me that there is no harm in it! You're too low down for me.

I want to see the color of some buck's hair that can dance with my wife! I'm going to monopolize that hugging myself.

Do you know that three-fourths of all the girls who are ruined owe their downfall to that very thing. You let a young man whose character would make a black mark on a piece of tar paper, who goes down the line every other night, hug and dance with your daughter, and see what happens. They are dancing the tango, the rottenest, most putrid, stinkingest dance that ever wriggled out of the pit of perdition—that's what the tango is.

DO YOU WATCH YOUR DAUGHTER DANCE?

Are you a father? Are you a brother? Do you accompany your daughter or your sister to the ballroom and see young fellows come up to her—lecherous young bucks—asking the hand of your daughter or your sister for a dance—young bucks that you know live in sin, young fellows whose names are as common upon the lips of the prostitute as upon the lips of your daughter. Two or three nights in company with her at some ball or theater party and two or three nights in the arms of some prostitute. You stand there and see young fellows come up and walk with your daughter and tell me that there is no harm in it. You are too low down for me.

Are you a mother? And do you chaperon your daughter and groom her, and you shove here in front of every marriageable buck, and you accompany her to the ballroom and you stand there and look at her with your head cocked on one side, and see a young fellow come up and wrap his arms around your daughter, and tell me that there is no harm in it? You must be made out of basswood or putty or marble ….

When I danced on the puncheon floor in the log cabin on the frontier in Iowa we used to be able to get a stick of wood between them, but now you can't get a piece of tissue paper between them. We're going some nowadays. I can understand why some of the young people want to dance, but what some of you old fellows who have to grease your joints before going on the floor see in it I don't know.

I read the other day that sitting out in a waltz is going to be fashionable from now on. The only difference is that you will sit it out instead of dance it. A young man and a girl will sit on a sofa, and he will put his right arm about her, and her left hand in his, and she rests her head upon his bosom, and all that they have to do is just to sit there and 'hug.' I tell you that there is some sense in that. I have always considered it a nuisance to gallop a mile just to get a hug or two.

Most men don't care a rap for the dance; it is the hug that they are after. That'll give your old rheumatic and gout masters a chance. A fellow has got to get powerfully old and decrepit when he doesn't enjoy a hug. I'll tell you that.

I want to tell you I don't believe that there are many people who can go on the ballroom floor and dance with a pretty girl hugged to his breast and look upon her charms under the influence of fascinating music and then go out with prayer-meeting feelings. I will bet you, sir, if men who dance would tell the truth 90 out of 100 will say:

You are right, Bill; you are the first one who ever had the grit to tell it.

Professor Faulkner, chairman of the Dancing Masters Association on the Coast, who had six private dancing schools of his own, and an income of a thousand dollars a month, was converted and gave them up, and if there was no harm in it, why not keep on?

I have more respect for a saloon keeper than for a dancing teacher.

I don't believe the saloons will do as much to damn the morals of young people as the dancing school.

That is my position. I don't care anything about yours.

Professor Faulkner said that he knew of one private dancing school that sent six girls into houses of ill fame in about three months. He talked with 200 girls and found that 165 fell as the result of the dance, 20 by drink, 10 by choice and 7 from poverty.

Where do you find the accomplished dancers? In the brothels. Why? They were taught in dancing schools....

SOLUTION OF THE SOCIAL EVIL

And while we're on the subject of prostitution, I think the best way to deal with the problem is to segregate all the prostitutes to one part of the city. Let everyone certify as to the house they are in on a certain date, their name, age, where they are from, the color of their hair and eyes. Not allow them to move from one house to another, unless the police know of it, and keep them off the streets except at certain hours. There are a lot of crank reformers who haven't got horse sense and do more injury than good. I don't know if I have much, but think it over. If you don't agree with me, it doesn't cost you anything.

Sisters, if you countenance the dance you are your sister's murderess ....
No wonder that the world is not being brought to Jesus Christ ....
Don't talk about it; think what you can do for the world and God's truth!

You say it has never injured you? Then stop before it does. If I come back one year from tonight, some of you might not be able to say that ….Oh, the things that Christ will do for us if we yield ourselves to him? How many of you will say, "I'll live for Jesus—I'll give my heart to Him?"

NOTES

1. "Sunday Preaches Twice His Famous Sermon Denouncing Certain Amusements," *Baltimore Sun*, April 1, 1916, 6.
2. The *Boston Globe* reported that the total collections for Sunday's most recent campaigns in Boston, Philadelphia, Detroit, and Baltimore were respectively $66,225.71, $52,692.06, $48,289.70, and $45,032.73, totaling $212,240.20 or $4.26 million in today's value. "Sunday Takes In $9,599 a Week in Boston Town," *Democrat and Chronicle*, January 2, 1917, 18. Laurence L. Winship, "Sunday Scores Spiritualism," *Boston Globe*, December 29, 1916, 1.
3. Carl Sandburg, "Billy Sunday," *Poems for the People* (Chicago: Ivan R. Dee, 1999) 104–108.
4. "Labor Criticizes Sunday," *New York Times*, May 2, 1917, 7.

CHAPTER FOUR

"Why Princeton Did Not Ask Billy Sunday"

ANDREW WEST

April 1915
Princeton, New Jersey[1]

Like most touring orators of his day, Billy Sunday preached from a set of stock sermons using the same illustrations, organizations, and themes but altering small details to fit the locale. The same sermon he preached in Baltimore in 1916, he had preached in Philadelphia the year before.[2]

Princeton University was the first Presbyterian college in the American Colonies, predating the American Revolution. Billy Sunday identified himself as a Presbyterian (after becoming smitten with his future, well-heeled wife and cradle-Presbyterian Helen Thompson). So the Princeton Dean of the Graduate School, Andrew F. West, felt compelled to explain why the school was not officially endorsing Sunday's 1915 Philadelphia campaign.

How would you characterize West's objection? Compare his objections to Sandburg's and the Labor Forum's. *What is missing in all their critiques?*

Princeton University is being attacked in certain religious papers for not inviting Mr. Sunday to address our students. As a member of the Presbyterian Church and a teacher in Princeton University for over thirty years, may I ask, in view of recently published criticisms, that you will print this statement giving some of the reasons why Mr. Sunday was not invited to hold his meetings here under the auspices and with the endorsement of the university?

Let me say emphatically that it was not because Mr. Sunday's teachings are evangelical. Far from it, Princeton was founded and has lived on the fundamental, historical, evangelical Christian faith, and with few exceptions, no other gospel has been heard here. The attitude of President Hibben and the authorities is in accord with this, no matter what passing difficulties may arise.

Nevertheless, there are grave reasons why Princeton University should not favor Mr. Sunday's methods as likely to do good to our students. He has been free to come, as he did, and our students have been entirely free to hear him, and they did in large numbers—but not on invitation nor with the encouragement of the authorities of the university. Why not? Let me state some of the reasons:

1. In matters of religion there is only one standard for Christians, and that standard is our Lord and Savior Jesus Christ. I gladly admit that Mr. Sunday means to be evangelical in his statements. But many of his utterances are, to put it mildly, not Christlike, and some of them are travesties of the teaching of Christ. Take the following samples, less vulgar than many others, which are both a caricature and a perversion of one of the most sacred scenes in the New Testament:

> Mary was one of those sort of Uneeda biscuit, peanut butter, gelatin and pimento sort of women,

> Martha was a beefsteak, baked potato, apple sauce with lemon and nutmeg, coffee and whipped cream, apple pie and cheese sort of women.

> So you can have your pick, but I speak for Martha. So the churches have a lot of Marthas and a lot of Marys—merely bench warmers. Hurrah for Martha!

> So Martha was getting dinner and poked her head in the door were Mary was sitting and said:

> "Mary, caress thou not that I serve alone?"

> Wouldn't it make you tired if you were doing all the work and had your hands all over dough and sweat rolling off as you cooked the potatoes, if your big, lazy sister was sitting down doing nothing? Then Jesus said:

> "Tut, tut, Martha, thou carest for too many little things."

> Take another and worse instance, where Christ in prayer is turned to a jesting use:

> And as he prayed the fashion of His countenance was altered. Ladies, do you want to look pretty If some of you women would spend less on dope, pazaza, and cold cream, and get down own your knees and pray, God would make you prettier.

> Very funny, no doubt, and very blasphemous.

2. At times Mr. Sunday is irreverently familiar toward God. This appears clearly in the scene at his Philadelphia meeting on Jan. 8:

> Why if I thought I could get any nearer God by kneeling, or get nearer to Him by taking off my coat, I'd do it.

(here Sunday suited the action to the word and tore off his coat form his back. Seizing it by the collar in his right have, he flung it around to lend emphasis to his utterances.)

Here is another sample:

> When I am at heaven's gate, I'll be free from old Philly's blood. I can see now the Day of Judgment, when the question of Philadelphia and of me is taken up by God.
>
> "You were down in Philly, weren't you, Billy?" the Lord will ask me.
>
> And I'll say to Him," Yes, Sir, Lord, I was there."
>
> "Did you give them my message of salvation, Billy?"
>
> "I gave them your message, Lord. I gave it to them the best way I could and as I understood it. You go get the files of the Philadelphia papers. They printed my sermons, Lord. You'll see in them what I preached," will be my answer."
>
> And the Lord will say, "Come on in, Bill; you're free from Philadelphia's blood."

Is this the way the Bible speaks? There is no place in that book for swaggering impiety. "Enter not into judgment with thy servant, O Lord," is the right attitude of should in the presence of God. Mr. Sunday is speaking impudently in the presence of "the King eternal, immortal, and invisible" to whom alone is due "honor and glory forever"—even now, ever at Mr. Sunday's performances. It was Jonathan Edwards, an early President of Princeton, who wrote of these sublime words in hushed awe as he gazed from his window one Autumn day: "As I read them the whole forest seemed to glow." No irreverence there. Is not the devout fear of God the "beginning of wisdom" still, and is it not deeply needed in American life today?

3. Many of Mr. Sunday's remarks are personally abusive or disgusting or slanderous. Take without comment the following series:

> If a woman on the avenue plays a game of cards in her home, she is worse than any blackleg gambler in the slums.
>
> If a minister believes and teaches evolution, he is a stinking skunk, a hypocrite, and a liar.
>
> If I were the wife of some of you men, I'd refuse to clean their old spittoons. I say let every hog clear his own trough.

Your wife is as good a right to line up before a bar and fill up her skin with the hog gut you do as you have.

Do we need more of the same sort?

4. There are also some statements, fortunately few—but enough which are plainly indecent. Take the following instances and remember they are the words of a professed minister of the Gospel of Christ spoken at a so-called religious service. See if you approve of them:

I can understand why young bloods go in for dancing, but some of you old ginks—goodnight.

Ma and I stopped in to look at a ball at an inauguration ceremony. Well, I will be horn-swoggled if I didn't see a woman there dancing with all the men, and she wore the collar of her gown around her waist. She had a little corset on—oh, I can't describe it!

You stand there and watch man after man as he claims her hand and puts his name on her list. Perhaps that fellow was her lover and you won her hand—and you stand there and watch your wife folded in his long, voluptuous, sensual embrace, their bodies swaying one against the other, their limbs twinning and entwining, her head resting on his breast, they breathe the vitiated air beneath the glittering candelabra and the spell of the music, and you stand there and tell me that there is no harm in it! You're too low down for me.

I want to see the color of some buck's hair that can dance with my wife! I'm going to monopolize that hugging myself.

Then Herodias came in and danced with her foot stuck out to a quarter to 12, and old Herod said, "Sis, you're a peach. You can have anything you want, even to the half of my kingdom." She hiked off to her licentious mother.

Why, a man with red blood in his veins can't look at half the women on the street now, and not have impure thoughts.

Little girl, you look so small.
Don't you wear no clothes at all?
Don't you wear no chemise shirt?
Don't you wear no petty skirt?
Don't you wear no underclothes,
But your corset and your hose?
No decent person can read these quotations without shame.

Every passage quoted in this article is taken from the official copyrighted report of Mr. Sunday's Philadelphia addresses, published with his sanction in *The Philadelphia Evening Telegraph* during January and February. Their accuracy cannot be questioned. It is true that these quotations are not the main stock and substance of his addresses, but some of the occasional ornaments, giving what is called "punch" to his discourses. They are things of the sort singled out for special separate printing in the *Evening Telegraph*, often in large type, as "jolts." So they are.

So in the name of decency and of the purity and sanctity of our Christian faith Princeton University positively refuses to approve Mr. Sunday's performances as suitable for the edification of our students. In times of hysterical excitement, we think it our right and duty to stand firm against all inflammatory mob-oratory in whatever field it may appear. For his quiet and sensible stand in this matter, President Hibben deserves the thanks for all friends of education and religion.

NOTES

1. Andrew F. West, "Why Princeton Did Not Ask Billy Sunday: A Statement in Defense of the Inhospitable Attitude of the University Authorities Toward that Evangelist," *New York Times*, April 8, 1915, 12.
2. "'You Can't Sow Sin and Reap Virtue,' Roars Sunday in His Attacks on Modern Dancing," *Williamsport Sun-Gazette*, February 13, 1915, 5. The text available in these 1915 Pennsylvania papers is incomplete compared to the Baltimore version.

CHAPTER FIVE

"Modern Woman"

BOB JONES, SR.

Marshall, Texas
March 28, 1924[1]

Robert Reynolds Jones' influence as a mover-and-shaker in conservative Evangelicalism is profound. While Billy Sunday had bigger and more lucrative revivals, Bob Jones' choice to start a high school and junior college for "One-Hundred-Percent Americans" along the coast of Florida would guarantee his influence into the twenty-first century. Just as his only son was ready to enter high school in 1927, Jones founded Bob Jones College, which would eventually settle in Greenville, South Carolina (after a stint in the hills of Tennessee) with the new moniker, Bob Jones University. BJU is infamously known as the institution of higher learning which, in 1983, under the umbrella of "religious freedom," defended its white nationalist idea that races should not intermarry in the ominously named Supreme Court case, The People of the United States v. Bob Jones University.*

BJU would lose that 1983 fight and their tax exemption since they refused to cast aside their racial hierarchy despite social pressure. Rhetors still reference that case as we continue to interrogate religious institutions' refusal to acknowledge the rights of other marginalized groups.

But Bob Jones University's recalcitrant ideas about white supremacy were not a new development in the 1980s. That institution has a clear ideological genealogy dating back decades. Along with a clear separation of the races, BJU, BJC, and all the men named Bob Jones—III, Junior, and Senior—looked askance at immigrants while presuming that liquor and other vices should not only be avoided but also outlawed for all Americans.

Jones' most consistent dramatistic antagonist, however, is startling. Of course, Jones frames everyone outside his inner circle as thwarting American progress. That's expected. Foreigners, non-Protestants, and political adversaries all act in a way that disgusts and stymies Jones. In 1911—just months before his only son would be born to his second wife—Bob Jones first preached about his most dastardly opponent: The Modern Woman. This sermon for women-only would be his most frequently preached from 1911 through 1932. By 1923 he had intensified the problems of the modern woman with abortion and underworld references. When he preached this sermon in Atlanta in 1912, Jones claimed that he could be more "direct, personal, and intimate" with only women listening, so even the "ushering and taking up of the offering will be placed in the hands of the ladies." "I mean to talk very frankly," he claimed to encourage attendance.[2]

The sermon met a lot of controversy, not only from women but also from fellow ministers. Rev. Hugh Robinson Bernard, well-known Georgia Baptist,[3] criticized Bob's sermon explicitly for his maligning of the "mantle of charity" modern women "throw" "about the shoulders of an erring sister."[4]

Jones' "Modern Woman" might be a woman of color or a white woman, middle-aged or young, upper or working class. Any female who calls herself out of the shadows and into action—any woman who acts—receives Jones' ire. These women flamboyantly sin for their own pleasure and lead God's greatest civilization, America, right to hell. Consistently, Jones frames women as the second persona in his rhetoric. They are "crying women" who have as much civic power in their tears as Jones has in casting his ballot. They are "running" all the spheres. Jones' moralism is political, not spiritual.

In 2014, the evangelical organization Godly Response to Abuse in the Christian Environment (GRACE) published a report summarizing Bob Jones University's mishandling of sexual assault on their campus. The investigators cited this 1911 sermon as proof of the century-long misogyny that undergirded that mishandling. Thus, white nationalism persists in casting aspersions on women who act. For Jones, a woman's job is only to support the hierarchy as it exists. Good women are lovely vessels on a shelf that are never used and only appreciated when they are displayed. How is Jones' description of the "modern woman" parallel to Sunday's description of immorality? How are their actors similar? Does Princeton's, Sandburg's, and Labor's critique do enough? How should we counter their white nationalism?

As a rule, great women are the daughters of great men, but whenever a great man touches this earth, back of him was a great mother. This mother may have lived in obscurity, but you may rest assured that whenever you see a great man in any walk of life, that man had a great mother.

From a human standpoint the hope of the world has been the goodness of women. Men have always been bad, but women had to some extent at least counteracted the depravity of depraved men as generations have been born into this world. No nation ever went to ruin until the women of that nation became corrupt. All the forces of evil can never destroy America if our women remain pure.

In the sight of God the sin of man and the sin of woman is the same. Any sin that will damn a woman will damn a man. God makes no distinction. While this is true, the consequences of a woman's sin in this world are more serious than the sin of man. In other words, if all men were corrupt, and all women were pure, I would still have some hope for the world, but if all women were corrupt, and all men were pure, I could have no hope for the future of the human race.

I am sorry to say to you that in my lifetime I have seen a change take place the women of this country. Do not misunderstand me, I have not lost faith in women. A man is far on the road to ruin when he loses confidence in all women. But I must be true to you, and say I think the percentage of good men in this country maybe on the increase, but I fear the percentage of good women is on the decrease. Women are still better than men, but if certain tendencies with which we are going to deal in this address are not checked, the women will not always be better than the men. I sometimes feel that in view of some conditions in our modern life I had rather have a responsibility of rearing a boy then a girl.

Woman in this country has come down from the pedestal where men admired her twenty-five years ago.

Men are losing respect for women as a whole. You take the nicest girl in the city and let her get aboard a railroad train and start on a journey. It would be surprising if she should reach the end of her journey without some wicked man on the train attempting to flirt with her. Why is that? The average man of the world knows that he can flirt with so many women he is willing to take chances with any of them. A few years ago even a wicked, malicious man would not dare flirt with a strange woman, but the godless, giddy, flippant and loud girls and women of this country have dragged down all women in the estimation of a great many men. It is a sad day for our world when men lose respect for women.

You will find my text in First Timothy, the fifth chapter and the six verse: "but she that liveth in pleasure is dead while she liveth."

Now let's study for just a few minutes the effects and results of this fashion craze. In the first place, let's look at the effect upon the woman herself. God gave you a soul, a mind, and a body. Your soul is the highest part of your being. Your mind is next, your body is the lowest part of your being. The whole tendency of the modern craze is to concentrate the attention on the body. There was a time when men saw women they looked up. Now they look down. The tendency is to catch the attention of men and concentrate this attention altogether on the body. There are many of you women in this audience who are nothing more or less than decorated animals. You live on the animal plane. There is where you think.

There are mothers here who take their girls when they are young and innocent and consecrate these girls on the altar of fashion. The girls in this country who ought to have roses of modesty blooming in their cheeks have their faces covered with paint. They are old before they are grown. Many of them are loud, and immodest, and you can't expect anything else.

EXTRAVAGANCE IN DRESS

There is not only the immodesty of the dress, there is the extravagance. There is the effect of extravagance on the home life in America. Some of you women listening to me now have your husband's nose to the grindstone and you are turning the grindstone. There are men whose wives are in this service who are out in the business world sweating blood to pay for the expensive clothes that you wear to your social functions. There are men in the penitentiary today who would never have been there if they had been married to economical, practical, sensible women. If a worldly, extravagant, flippant butterfly of a wife drives a man to crookedness in business by her extravagance, she ought to be put behind the bars in the place of her husband, and he ought to be hung for being a fool.

Listen to me, ladies, the sin of America today is the sin of impurity. The battle that confronts the American manhood and womanhood is the fight for personal purity. I sometimes speak on the text, "They have eyes full of adultery." I wish I had time to preach that sermon to you women. I tell you this much. The immodest dress of women has had more to do with filling the eyes of men with impurity than any other one influence. I tell you frankly I have ceased to hope for men to live pure as long as women dress indecently.

The way to break up this street mashing is easy. Just let the women in this country go back to their old-time modest street dresses, and you will soon disperse that crowd of degenerates.

THE BOSSY WIFE

Another thing about the type of women I am discussing, she is inclined to be "bossy." When you and your husband married, you had one room and one bureau. You said, "Now, dearie, you take this drawer and I will take this one." In a few weeks you crowded him out of his bureau space and suggested to him that he must get a chiffonier or chifforobe, just for himself. It wasn't long till you crowded him out of chiffonier space. You wanted to run the home and take possession of everything. Homes are not planned for women and girls. Your husband went uptown and got an office, and it wasn't long until his stenographer was running that. You women have been running the Church for a number of years and now you are going to run the Government.

I tell you frankly I never was for women suffrage. I was afraid of the tendency.

I am willing for you to run the home, the business world, the church and the government, but I don't like for you to be so "bossy" about it.

When God gave a woman the privilege of becoming a mother and rearing a family. He gave her the greatest honor and the greatest opportunity for service that He every conferred upon a human being.

DON'T IMITATE MEN

I despise a bossy woman, who wants to be like a man. I don't think a "sissy" man is as unattractive as a "buddy" woman. You can't be a man. You needn't try. God made you different. God made your voice different. He made you voice to sing lullabies to a baby. He gave a man a voice so he could go out in the field and call the hogs. He gave you a dainty hand so you could pin the clothes and tie ribbons on the baby. He gave a man big hands to harness the horse and drive the cattle from the field. He gave you a fountain for the nourishment of your baby. When I say that some of these modern girls blush. If anything makes me tired, it is to see some girl who exposes her form to the gaze of human society and then throws up her hands in holy horror at a good old-time American mother who nurses her baby in the old-time way.

Another thing about the type of woman I am discussing, she is lax in her ideals. In the old days with the old-time woman everything was black or white. Now things are a dull gray. The colors have come together. Here is what I mean: years ago if a woman had a bad name you kicked her out of society. Now you elect her president of a club. I can remember when a woman was divorced she was disgraced, but now she is one of the shining lights of society. I, of course, understand that the Bible gives one ground for divorce, but remember, there is only one. If your husband is untrue to you, you are entitled to a divorce according to the Bible.

If a girl can be crooked and keep her social position, society puts a premium on crookedness. The girls of the community say, "I don't have to be good. Look at Miss So-and-So. She does as she pleases and she is the most popular girl in town." I believe in the old method of casting them out when they are not straight.

Now do not misunderstand me. I am not talking about the women of the underworld. I have been down to those homes of sin where the lights of impurity were burning, where those soiled doves lived in their earthly hell. I have been there to take the gospel to them. I have told them God loved them, and I have seen the tears of penitence cut trenches in the paint on their faces. I have seen them weep their way into the arms of God. I stand ready to help those women. I would befriend them, try to get them on their feet, and secure for them an opportunity to make an honest living. The woman that I want to see cast out is the impenitent, brazen, shadowed society woman who sometimes is as crooked in the sight of God as a woman of the underworld, but who keeps her social position and lifts in society her defiant head and thinks she is as good as the best.

Several years ago, I was talking to a prominent lawyer who is on the supreme bench of one of our southern states. This gentleman said, "Bob Jones, if the women do not quit reading the sex novels that are now being circulated among them, the purity of the womanhood of this country will soon be gone." I have stood on many a streetcar and have seen some girl holding onto a strap and absorbed in some book that I personally would blush to read.

MODERN WOMAN PLEASURE LOVER

The Modern Woman is more and more becoming a pleasure lover. They go to theaters, they play cards, and they dance.

I think the histrionic talent is as God-given as any other talent, but I have long since learned that the devil has a mortgage on the American theater.

The stage is the only place where a person does not have character to get by.

We have reached a terrible day in our history when moving-picture actors and actresses who have been divorced and whose names have been connected with all kinds of scandal have become the ideal and teachers of our boys and girls.

All of these pictures and play filled with kissing scenes and suggestive plots have had much to do with the pulling down of the barriers between the sexes and have contributed much to the production of the loud, immodest type of girl we have today.

CARD PLAYING

Another thing about the type of woman I am discussing, she is a card fiend. There is something about a deck of cards which cannot be made decent, though it is shuffled by the jeweled fingers of a church society woman. There is the odor of a gambling hell about every deck of cards you ever saw. The spades tell of graves they have dug in every cemetery. The clubs speak to us of heads they have crushed, and the hearts bring to our memory the human hearts they have broken, yet there are church women who are listening to me now who are as much intoxicated with card playing as any drunkard was ever intoxicated with drink. Some of you women go to bed at night and in your dreams you see the cards. You go to church on Sunday morning and while you are trying to listen to the sermon you see a deck of cards before your face ....

THE MODERN DANCE

The modern woman manifests her love for pleasure by participating in the modern dance. The dance has reached such a point nobody with any brains attempts to defend it. Even the dancing masters of American have been expressing themselves freely about the immodesty and indecency of the dance in which most of the young people and some of the older people of American are taking part. You women needn't think that you can make dances decent with had their beginning in the underworld.

I do not say all girls have evil thoughts when they dance. I know that there are some girls who go through life without ever having any real evil thoughts and impulses. This is not true, however, with all girls.

I tell you why you women let your daughters dance. Every married woman here knows that there is a danger lurking in the whirl and music and familiarity of a ballroom. You let your daughter dance because you have confidence in her, and you want her to be popular in the community. I tell you that you do not know what kind of devil sleeps in the blood of your child.

The mother who does not welcome her child when he is born, deserves to be cursed by that child when he is grown. I don't say the child ought to curse the mother, but the mother deserves to be cursed.

Let me plead with you women. Turn your back on these questionable, sordid things of the work. Dedicate your hands to God. Lift up the flag of purity. Hold true to the traditions handed down to you from the old-time women of this country. Dedicate your life unreservedly to Jesus Christ, the Son of God. He's a woman's friend. He took the chains of slavery from your hand, and made you a queen. You owe your liberty and your all to Him. Come clean with him today.

NOTES

1. "Bob Jones Preaches to 2,000 Women on the Modern Woman," *Marshall Messenger*, March 29, 1924, 1 and 6. "Thousands of Women Hear Bob Jones Paint Picture in Words of Modern Women," *Marshall Morning News*, March 29, 1924, 1–3.
2. "Bob Jones Will Speak to Women Only Sunday," *The Atlanta Constitution*, June 01, 1912, 16.
3. Charles Jones, "Athens Ministers Led Way for Baptist Giving," *Athens Banner-Herald*, July 14, 2004. https://www.onlineathens.com/article/20140717/LIFESTYLE/307179984/.
4. "Dr. H. R. Bernard replies to sermon of Rev. 'Bob' Jones," *The Atlanta Constitution*, June 4, 1912, 6.

PART 3

Naming America's White Nationalism

The 1924 Democratic National Convention was an event full of superlatives. Having received national suffrage four years earlier, women for the first time could join the men as delegates on the national stage. For the first time, the public could catch all the proceedings live on radio right in their living rooms. As far as individuals were concerned, Franklin Delano Roosevelt would for first time wield political influence since his polio diagnosis, and William Jennings Bryan would exercise his national influence for his last. The event also became known as the largest gathering of the Ku Klux Klan in the history of the organization, dubbed the "Klan Bake," in the New York press.[1] As the convention progressed delegates and candidates would identify as either for or against the infamous organization. William McAdoo, son-in-law to the recently deceased Woodrow Wilson, was the "Klandidate," and William Jennings Bryan led white Protestants to endorse him and refrain from condemning the Klan. McAdoo's chief contender was New York Governor Al Smith, a Catholic who was utterly perturbed by McAdoo's popularity among white Protestants. So as an alternative, Smith chose the Rabbi Stephen S. Wise to open the sixth convention session in prayer. Smith saw the Zionist as an alternative to Bryan. The cleric opened the session on Saturday at 4:00pm.[2]

> Almighty God and Father, give of Thy merciful guidance to this gathering of the Sons and Daughters of our beloved Nation, that together we may greatly serve the highest and noblest interests of our Country. Help us to be brotherly and forbearing to one another, but dauntlessly resolute for the right. May we battle for truth, not for advantage, for public honor and not private gain, for the privilege of service and not the glory of victory. Unless

the Lord build the house, they labor in vain who build it. So let this mighty gathering help to build the house of a righteous and peace-furthering Nation; and in the unity of our fellowship and the bond of our common devotion to our loved land may there be abiding and abounding fulfillment of the prophecy, "For Mine house shall be called an house of prayer unto all peoples." And Thine, Oh Father, be the honor and the praise and the glory, forevermore. Amen.

That day the Democrats debated the party platform, specifically over whether to officially condemn the Ku Klux Klan. Two speakers brought the house to cheers and boos. Andrew Cobb Erwin surprised everyone when he spoke against expectations and condemned the KKK. William Jennings Bryan, on the other hand, attempted an all-too-common appeal for the party to simply "return to Jesus" rather than condemn white supremacy. Bryan's speech especially perturbed Will Rogers who described that Saturday as "the day when I heard the most religion preached, and the least practiced of any day in the world's history."[3]

NOTES

1. The term first appears in Joseph A. Cowen's column in the New York *Daily News*. "Klanbake steamed open at 12:45. Only three bungstarters crippled in calling delegates to disorder." Cowen had little patience with the whole event, continuing: "Georgia klucks started Mc'll-doodle-do-o-o-kackle. 'This is no cold storage warehouse,' rumbled [Pat Harrison] the boy orator of the Mississipp' and the egg was sent back for more klandeling." "'Twas Pat Harrison's Corking Speech that Started the Conclave Vizzing," *New York Daily News*, June 25, 1924, 4.
2. Rabbi Stephen Wise, *Official Proceedings of the Democratic National Convention*, (Indianapolis: Walter, Ball, Greathouse Printing, 1924) 227.
3. Will Rogers, "North Carolina's Higher Mathematics Proves Too Much for Will Rogers," *Ithaca Journal News*, June 30, 1924.

CHAPTER SIX

"I Come from Georgia!"

ANDREW COBB ERWIN

New York City
June 28, 1924[1]

Among the flurry of religious rhetoric at the 1924 Democratic National Convention, one voice surprised the delegates. Just before Bryan, a son of a Confederate officer and former mayor of the Klan stronghold, Athens, Georgia, spoke. He looked frail. His voice cracked. But when he spoke outside the stereotype of a Southern politician and against *the Ku Klux Klan, Madison Square Garden erupted with both hisses and cheers. The official transcript of the convention documented that the audience interrupted Erwin four times with loud applause. When he was done, delegates from half the states "gathered round Mr. Erwin, cheering him wildly, and finally lifted him upon their shoulders and paraded around the hall" while the band played. The whole procession continued ten minutes until the Chairman banged the gavel for them to return to their seats. Amidst all those jeers and ovations, Andrew Cobb Erwin gave us a model of how to act within a politically charged religious climate.*

In October 2017 in the wake of the Charlottesville "Unite the Right" rally, Athens, Georgia held a town hall meeting to discuss its handling of their local memorials to the Confederacy. And Andrew Cobb Erwin's little three-minute speech from 1924 entered the 2017 civic conversation. His grandson Milton Leathers read it in the public library to remind his neighbors how to resist.[2] How would you describe Erwin's strategy? How do Agent and Act and Scene work together in his speech? What does Erwin have to say to us today? How can you imagine acting in a similar way in our current civic sphere?[3]

Ladies and gentlemen of the Convention: I am a delegate from Georgia. I am proud of it. To my mind, the Ku Klux issue is the most vital one which the Democratic Party has to determine. You have two courses that you may follow. You can, by adopting the report of the majority, evade the issue, which would, in effect, give your approval to the activities of this organization. Follow this course and you may prepare for an ignominious defeat at the polls in November. Meet the issue squarely, as the people of this Country expect you to meet it, and a glorious victory will be yours.

I come from Georgia, and we have been trying for five years to get you Yankees to talk about this proposition.

You hear on every side, in the lobbies of the hotels, in the halls, and upon the floor of this Convention, "that we should take no action relating to the Klan any more than we should take action relating to the Masons or Elks or any other secret organization." I cannot bring myself to this view of it; I have not heard of the Masons or Elks moving from State Convention to State Convention, from National Convention to National Convention, regardless of party, a highly paid staff of officials, lobbyists and spying investigators, with a view of controlling the acts of the delegates chosen to represent the people of this Country. And just so soon as they do, then I favor a plank denouncing them, or any other secret society, in as strong words as a human hand can write.

As has been so ably pointed out by the distinguished speakers who have addressed you, the Constitution of the United States guarantees every person in America the right to worship God according to the dictates of his own conscience. It insures equal protection to all citizens, regardless of race or religion. The Constitution of every State in the Union preserves to each individual the right of freedom of conscience. The Ku Klux Klan makes a direct attack on these vital principles of our fundamental law. Its insidious activities have spread discord and distrust throughout this land of peace and harmony. However worthy the motives of its adherents may be, it constitutes the most destructive element in America today. The time has passed to temporize with these misguided people. They have challenged every citizen who cherishes and respects the Constitution. I, for one, am ready to accept that challenge. I am a Protestant; I adhere to the tenets of that faith; but it would ill become me to deny to others that for which my ancestors fought. I come from a State that was founded as a haven for the oppressed, where all men might be free to breathe the air of religious liberty. I say that those Georgians who do not take a stand against this hooded menace, which prowls, in the darkness, that dares not show its face, is not worthy of his ancestry; and I call upon you, my fellow-Georgians, in this Convention, to vote for the minority report of the Committee, I call upon you, my fellow-delegates from the South, in the name of that hallowed Roman Catholic priest, Father Ryan, the Poet Laureate of the Southern Confederacy, whose deathless verse you learned at your mother's knee,

I call upon you in the name of that loyal Jewish Patriarch, Judah P. Benjamin, who stood steadfast by his chieftain, Jefferson Davis, even as the star of the Southern Confederacy was declining, to purge from your hearts this senseless prejudice. To my fellow-delegates from the entire Country I invoke the memory of those Americans of other races than your own who died with your own kindred on the fields of France. I implore my fellow-delegates from Georgia to vote with other delegates in this Convention to erase the stigma that has been placed upon our State. Let us show the world that no American worthy of the name will bend his knee to this un-American and unchristian thing.

Especially do I adjure you fellow-Georgians to speak out like the men and women I know you to be and to demonstrate that Georgia is still entitled to wear her ancient motto: "Wisdom, Justice, Moderation."

NOTES

1. Andrew Cobb Erwin, *Official Proceedings of the Democratic National Convention*. (Indianapolis: Walter, Ball, Greathouse Printing, 1924) 297–298.

2. Lee Shearer, "Moving Athens' Confederate Monument Finds Support at Library Gathering." *Athens Banner*. August 17, 2017, Accessed September 17, 2018. http://www.onlineathens.com/local-news/2017-08-17/moving-athens-confederate-monument-finds-support-library-gathering.

3. For a larger analysis of Andrew Cobb Erwin's speech, see Camille K. Lewis, "'I Come From Georgia!': Andrew Cobb Erwin's Southern Resistance to the Ku Klux Klan," *Rhetoric & Public Affairs 23*, no.2 (Summer 2020): 331–65.

CHAPTER SEVEN

"Jesus Is More Needed"

WILLIAM JENNINGS BRYAN

New York City
June 28, 1924[1]

William Jennings Bryan was a leading influence in the Democratic Party from 1896 until this 1924 Democratic National Convention. He had been Nebraska's 1ˢᵗ district Representative for two terms, the Party's presidential nominee three times, and Woodrow Wilson's Secretary of State from 1913 to 1915. A year after this speech, Bryan would defend Creationism at the infamous Dayton, Tennessee Scopes Trial in which he won the battle in the courtroom, but lost the war for conservative Protestantism's respectability in the civic sphere. Five days after Scopes, Bryan died in his sleep in Dayton, Tennessee.

But the Scopes Trial was still a year in the future. Here in June 1924, Bryan was a delegate from Florida, serving on the Platform committee. He had been quite an influence behind the scenes for Wilson's League of Nations, for McAdoo's nomination, and for, in this case, the Majority position—the position that did not *name the Ku Klux Klan in the plank on religious liberty. Because of the lengthy discussion over the platform that went into the wee hours of the morning, Bryan had received little sleep the night before this speech.[2]*

But according to historian Robert Murray, the young upstart Andrew Cobb Erwin especially incensed Bryan. During Erwin's short speech, Bryan "was furiously scribbling notes," and, Murray remembers, had been Erwin's age when he brought the house down with his "Cross of Gold" speech in 1896.[3]

Even though Bryan asked the audience to not applaud since he would lose speaking minutes, the applause and the hisses and boos interrupted him nearly thirty times. After the fourth paragraph, the official proceedings state there were "long and continued hisses, boos, and jeers." After three raucous interruptions, Chair David Walsh stated, "If the speaker is again interrupted by the galleries, they will be cleared. (Applause and some hisses.) I shall order this in the name of the delegates that this speaker is to continue, and without interruption from them." All further interruptions were only applause—until his last sentence: "And, my friends, we can exterminate Ku Kluxism better by recognizing their honesty and teaching them that they are wrong."

Notice the dichotomies Bryan offers in his address: Protestant vs. Catholic, religion vs. greed, Democrat vs. Republican, common folk vs. monopolists, Old Testament patriarchs vs. delegates, political platforms vs. Jesus. How does his framing attempt to alter the conversation? With those plain dichotomies, who is the agent in Bryan's drama? What action is that agent doing?

Mr. Chairman, ladies and gentlemen, members of the Convention: It is now twenty-eight years since Democratic Conventions became gracious enough to invite me and patient enough to listen to me, and I have not words in which to express my gratitude for the love and loyalty of millions of Democrats who have been my co-laborers for more than a quarter of a century. I have spoken to you on many themes, never on themes more important that this today, and since they take applause out of my time, and since I am speaking to your hearts and heads and not to your hands, keep still and let me speak to you.

I have only a short time in which to lay before you the arguments that seem to me pertinent to this occasion, when we are about to decide not only the line of our campaign this Fall, but questions which may affect larger things than parties.

Let's understand each other. Let's eliminate the things that are not in this issue and come down to the three words that these, our good friends, as honest, as patriotic and as anxious for the welfare of the party as we are, take out of the language and exalt above any other three words that will be used in this campaign. Note, my friends, that they take our report, every word of it, and not also that we offered to take every word of their report but three. We said, "Strike out three words and there will be no objection." But three words were more to them than the welfare of a party in a great campaign.

You have listened to the applause when we had had read to you the best Democratic platform that was ever written, the noblest principles that have been written into a platform. We have their pleas pathetic for people in distress, but none of our principles, none of our pleas stirred the hearts of these men like the words, "Ku Klux Klan."

I call you to witness that these men never took the standards of their States and marched when we appealed on grand principles; it was only when they said "Ku Klux Klan," that's the only thing.

Citizens of New York, you show your appreciation of the honor we did you in holding our Convention here.

Let me place before you the five reasons which I submit to your judgments and your consciences. First, this plank, these three words, are not necessary.

There is not a State in the Union where anybody whose rights are denied cannot go and find redress, not a State in the Union; and the Democratic Party in its platform, the part of it on which we all agree, in words as strong as can be written, with emphasis as great as can be employed, puts all the strength of a great party back of every right, and especially back of the right of religious liberty for which we stand, as well as those who call us cowards because we do not take three words with which they seek to conjure. It is not necessary, I repeat, first because the laws protect everyone.

Second, it is not necessary to protect any Church. I, my friends, have such confidence in the Catholic Church, which was for over a thousand years my mother church as well as yours.

It was the Catholic Church that took religion from its founder and preserved it, the only custodian, for over a thousand years. And when they did it for the Catholic, they did it for me and for every Protestant.

The Catholic Church, with its legacy of martyred blood and with all the testimony of its missionaries who went into every land, does not need a great party to protect it from a million men. The Jews do not need this resolution. They have Moses. They have Elijah. They have Elisha, who was able to draw back the curtain and show upon the mountain tops an invisible host greater than a thousand Ku Klux Klans. And both the Catholic Church and the Jewish Faith have their great characters today who plead for respect for them, and whose pleading is not in vain. It is not necessary, and, my friends, the Ku Klux Klan does not deserve the advertisement that you give them.

The minority, the fourteen members of our Committee who could not join with us in a report that would leave out those three magic and mystic words, have raised the Ku Klux Klan to a higher attitude than the Ku Klux Klan themselves ever raised their fiery cross. Mr. Colby tells you that this is a transient organization; that it will soon die. If that be true, then really, my friends, the motto of the minority ought to be, "Hurry up if you would see George; he is nearly gone."[4]

My friends, one objection that I have to making this issue the paramount issue of this campaign is that I am not willing to lift up the dying embers and start a prairie fire and carry this Klan into every Congressional District of the United States.

My third objection is that we have no moral right to let them divert us from as great a mission as our party ever had.

They say we are cowards. My friends, it requires more courage to fight the Republican Party than it does to fight the Ku Klux Klan. Here we have farmers driven into bankruptcy, a million driven from the farms in a single year. We find monopoly spreading. We find nearly every great line of industry in the control of gigantic combinations of capital. And while we have distress in this Country that cries aloud for relief, and while we have a war worn world across the Atlantic that needs our help and needs our guidance, these minority men say that we lack courage if we do a big work instead of starting out on a little hunt for something which is nearly dead and which will soon pass away.

You may call me a coward if you will, but there is nothing in my life to justify the charge that I am a coward. But, my friends, I would rather have the anathemas of these misguided Democrats than have to answer on Judgment Day for a duty disregarded and a trust deserted. Anybody can fight the Ku Klux Klan, but only the Democratic Party can stand between the common people and their oppressors in this land.

Then, I am not willing to bring discord into my party. The Democratic Party is united on all the economic issues. We have never been so united since I have known politics, and nobody has had more reason than I to regret discord. Now, when we are all united and all stand with a dauntless courage and enthusiasm never excelled, these people tell us that we must turn aside from these things and divide our party with a religious issue and cease to be a great political party. Why, they tell us that if we do not do so and so, the Democratic Party is going to lose a large number.

My friends, if the Democratic Party will lose a considerable number because it insists on being what it has been, how many will it lose if it tries to be what it has never been? The Democratic Party has never been a religious organization. The Democratic Party has never taken the side of one church against the other. The Democratic Party must remain true. It cannot surrender its right to exist and the mission that was given to it in the days of Jefferson, that it remained true to in the days of Jackson, and to which it was still loyal in the days of Woodrow Wilson.

But, my friends, I have left for the last what I regard as the greatest argument. If the Democratic Party is diverted from its duty, some other party will take up its task.

But no party that takes up a noble task will find its leaders in the gallery today.

I repeat that if our party is turned aside from its transcendent duty as champion of the rights of the masses, another party can take our place. Even if our party were destroyed, another party would grow up to do its work.

And now I want to tell you my last and strongest objection, and let the galleries scoff if they dare: I say I am not willing to divide the Christian Church when we ought to stand together to fight the battles of religion in this land.

My friends, I am not responsible for your opinions. I am for mine. I have tried to defend the Democratic Party because of all I owe to it. It took me up when I was ten years younger than any other man had been when he was nominated by a great party, and it found me in a Western State, farther West than it had ever gone before, and it gave me a million more votes than it had ever given any Democrat before, and it nominated me twice afterward, and I never had to use any money, and I had no organization. The Democratic Party has done more for me than for any other living man, and, my friends, I am grateful. I cannot express my gratitude. I can paraphrase the words that are familiar when I express my sentiments:

"Partisans, spare that party, touch not a single bough;
In youth it sheltered me, and I will protect it now."

But, my friends, much as I owe to my party, I owe more to the Christian Religion. If my party has given me the foundations of my political faith, my Bible has given me the foundations of a faith that has enabled me to stand for the right without stopping to count how many stood to take their share with me.

My father taught me that I could afford to be in a minority, but that I could not afford to be wrong on any subject. He believed in the Bible and in God, and he believed that that God stood back of every righteous cause with an arm strong enough to bring victory to his side. And that has been my faith. And my friends, I believe religion is of more importance than politics, and I believe the world needs now not so much to get into a fight between denominations as it does to get back to God and a sense of responsibility to God.

Burglars stole sixty-five million in a year and pickpockets stole nearly as much, and bank robbers and bandits took large sums; but the swindlers took two billions, ten times as much as all the people in the penitentiary took. Isn't it worthwhile, my friends, to unite the Christian Church in behalf of the Ten Commandments and the Sermon on the Mount, instead of dividing them into warring factions?

The world is coming out of the war, the bloodiest ever known. Thirty millions of human lives were lost, three hundred billions of property was destroyed, and the debts of the world are more than six times as great as they were when the first gun was fired.

My friends, how are you going to stop war? Oh, they say, commerce will do it. But commerce did not do it, and commerce reached its highest point just before the war began. They said education will do it. But education did not do it. Education reached its highest point just before the war began. Some say science will do it. But science did not do it, for science had reached the highest point just before the war began. Yes, my friends, science instead of preventing war, mixed the poisonous gas and made the liquid fire. It was science that made war so hellish that civilization was about to commit suicide. Science cannot do it. There is only one thing that can bring peace to the world, and that is the Prince of Peace. That is, my friends, the One who, when He came upon the earth, the angels sang, "On earth peace, good will toward men."

My friends, Jew and Gentile, Catholic and Protestant, stand for God, on whom all religion rests, and Protestant and Catholic stand for the Prince of Peace. Is it possible that now, when Jesus is more needed, I say the hope of the world—is it possible that at this time, in this great land, we are to have a religious discussion and a religious warfare? Are you going, my friends, to start a blaze that may cause you innumerable lives, sacrificed on the altar of religious liberty? I cannot believe it. I call you back in the name of our God; I call you back in the name of our party; I call you back in the name of the Son of God and Savior of the world. Christians, stop fighting, and let us get together and save the world from the materialism that robs life of its spiritual values.

It was Christ on the Cross who said, "Father, forgive them, for they know not what they do." And, my friends, we can exterminate Ku Kluxism better by recognizing their honesty and teaching them that they are wrong.

After Bryan was done, the delegates began to vote on the platform itself. In the end, after much arm-twisting within each state's delegations, the Democratic party voted 542 3/20ths in favor of the Majority position—the position that did not *name the Ku Klux Klan—and 541 3/20ths in favor of the Minority position. One vote.*

At 2:00 am on Sunday, June 29, 1924, Franklin Roosevelt moved to adjourn the session.[5]

NOTES

1. William Jennings Bryan, *Official Proceedings of the Democratic National Convention.* (Indianapolis: Walter, Ball, Greathouse Printing, 1924) 303–08.
2. Robert Keith Murray, *The 103ʳᵈ Ballot: Democrats and the Disaster in Madison Square Garden* (New York: Harper & Row Publishers, 1976), 145–47.
3. Murray, *The 103ʳᵈ Ballot,* 156–57.
4. King George V of the United Kingdom ruled the British empire through World War I during which his health turned for the worse after a fall from a horse. By 1925 he was diagnosed with chronic pulmonary disease. Kenneth Rose, *King George V* (London: Phoenix Press, 2000), 301, 344.
5. *Official Proceedings of the Democratic National Convention.* (Indianapolis: Walter, Ball, Greathouse Printing, 1924) 334.

PART 4

Separating within America Itself

By World War 2, American Protestants had distanced themselves from the overt white supremacist rhetoric of the Ku Klux Klan and instead mixed the same ideology within other political anxieties. Appeals to piety persisted and xenophobia remained. As African Americans organized their resistance to white nationalism through the Civil Rights movement, white Protestants grew increasingly belligerent. Five rhetors demonstrate these statements and counter-statements. William Ward Ayer pastored the same Calvary Baptist Church in Manhattan as John Roach Straton. At the opening meeting of the conservative National Association of Evangelicals, he articulates an anti-immigrant message that sounds as klannish as revivalists twenty years earlier. By the 1950s, *Christianity Today* published an editorial from a well-degreed theologian, E. Earle Ellis, which sounds no different from Henry Grady and John Roach Straton. Billy James Hargis has none of the same pedigree or education, but in the Plains and across the West, he fought Communism with the same crusade against vice that Sunday used to combat liquor and Jones used to deride women. The last two rhetors end the 1960s in a head-to-head match. African American SNCC activist James Forman publicly read a "Black Manifesto" in 1969 that would inspire Bible Presbyterian founder Carl McIntire's own "Christian Manifesto."

CHAPTER EIGHT

"Evangelical Christianity Endangered by Its Fragmentized Condition"

WILLIAM WARD AYER

St. Louis
April 7, 1942[1]

In 1924 at Second Imperial Klonvokation in Kansas City, Missouri, the KKK's Imperial Wizard H. W. Evans delivered a speech called, "The Klan of Tomorrow." After explaining that the "Celts," the "Alpines," the "Slavs," the "Mediterraneans," and, unsurprisingly, the Jews all "[weaken] our Americanism," he states that the Ku Klux Klan is one *with Protestantism:*

> The Klan is Protestantism personified. In it are drawn together Protestants of all creeds—united in one body, for the defense and spread of those great principles which underlie the religious freedom guaranteed by the American Constitution. Protestantism is bigger than any creed.

> This unity between Protestantism and Americanism is no accident. The two spring from the same racial qualities, and each is a part of our group mind. Together they worked to build America, and together they will work to preserve it. Americanism provides politically the freedom and independence Protestantism requires in the religious field.[2]

After the 1924 Klan Bake and the disaster of that convention for the Democratic party, however, this explicit melding of Protestantism and white nationalism moved underground. William Ward Ayer is a rhetorical bridge between these overt and the covert strategies. Canadian-born conservative Evangelical Ayer pastored Manhattan's independent Calvary Baptist Church from 1936 through 1949. Ayer was on the Board of Regents for Billy James Hargis' American Christian College as well as on the Board of Trustees for Bob Jones University from 1942 until his death in 1985. In fact, Ayer's publishing house, Ayerow Christian Projects, continues to list its address at the Bob Jones University location in Greenville, South Carolina. While Ayer published a few book-length manuscripts such as Seven Saved Sinners *and* The Sure Word of Prophecy, *there is a single book listed as published by Ayerow:* The White Race: God's Most Successful Servant.

In April 1942, in St. Louis a new gathering of conservative Evangelicals began the National Association of Evangelicals. The group still exists today under the mission, "to honor God by connecting and representing evangelical Christians" in ecclesiology and public policy. [3] *In their opening meeting, however, after co-founders J. Elwin Wright and Harold Ockenga described the historical trajectory for starting the parachurch organization, their melding with white nationalism was plain. Ayer begins his address describing the present condition in the United States for conservative Evangelicals. His is a treacherous scene with much "hardship" and suffering. America itself was fragmented and antagonistic to Ayer and his tribe. While the counter-agent of the Federal Council of Churches and the federal government threaten "independent" religious radio broadcasters like Ayer, the most ominous counter-agents are foreign influences—immigrants coded under the term "Marxists." White "evangelism," he explains, would preserve "American-ism."*

In essence, no difference exists between Ayer's argument against foreigners and the Klu Klux Klan, nor between Henry Grady, John Roach Straton, Frances Willard, Billy Sunday, or Bob Jones. The melding of the white nationalism and conservative Evangelicalism persists. How would Kenneth Burke imagine a comic corrective to this persistence? How can we casuistically stretch the boundaries of religious arguments in the public sphere to accommodate neighborliness and kindness?

Perilous times confront the Christian Church. Difficulties loom in the path ahead. Evangelical religion has suffered much in totalitarian countries, and it takes no great prophetic vision to see that in our own nation tendencies are developing which in due time will work considerable hardship upon unorganized Christianity.

We have great faith in our God's ability to deliver and lead His people, and it implies no lack of trust in God to clearly note the exigencies of the hour. It is my responsibility to awaken your minds to the dangers inherent in evangelical Protestantism's divided and fragmentized condition.

I. OUR FRAGMENTIZED CONDITION IS DANGEROUS TO A GENUINE EVANGELICAL TESTIMONY TO THE WORLD

Organizational unity is neither desirable nor necessary. Unanimity in religious things is only in church totalitarianism. The boast of evangelical Christianity is its liberty of thought, freedom of expression, and the right to differ, especially on non-essentials. But, if there cannot be unanimity, there must be unity, even in division. We must find a common meeting place for common purposes. There must be a hub in which the spokes of our several organizations can meet in order to make for firmness of purpose and service, and for solidarity in testimony.

There is certainly a common doctrinal ground upon which we all stand, and we occupy common spheres of activity, giving testimony to a glorious Christ in a lost world.

II. THERE ARE DANGERS TO OUR ORGANIZATIONAL EXISTENCE BECAUSE OF MODERN ATTITUDES OF GOVERNMENT

Ours is a day of regimentation. Everyone is being counted; everybody labeled; everybody signed up. Soon everybody will be classified. As America advances further into some form of "statism," let us not be deceived into believing that religion will escape. Governmental regimentation and classification in religion has ever been deadly to its free expression and growth. It has always tended to make the Church the inferior handmaiden of the state. It has circumscribed testimony, strangled evangelistic effort, and has set the religious life of nations into such rigid forms as to hinder its mobility.

Increasingly our government is demanding official representation for all national organizations and groups. Some have felt that we are not far from having a Minister of Religion in the President's Cabinet. Our government is becoming increasingly paternalistic and feels that it should direct the activities of all phases of our national life. It is coming to recognize only three great divisions in religion—Catholic, Jew, Protestant. It demands that there shall be official representatives of these three groups to function with government in its program. The Federal Council of the Churches of Christ in America steps forth and claims to be the official representative of all Protestant churches. The government, therefore, gladly does business with the Federal Council as representing Protestantism.

However, the Federal Council, though well organized, strong and competent in certain fields of religious activity, does not represent the great body of evangelical Christians in faith and doctrine. It claims to be the spokesman of twenty-two national churches, which is only forty percent of the total available. We feel sure that in doctrine and in many other matters it does not represent more than ten percent of this forty percent of the total denominational group. I would not deny the Federal Council its proper existence, but I feel that it does not represent me in many of its programs and pronouncements.

In the field of radio, the Federal Council of Churches and affiliated liberals control the free radio time assigned to Protestants upon two of the great networks, and is endeavoring to control the religious time upon local stations. Almost without exception they sponsor non-Gospel programs on the time allotted to them. There is not an outstanding evangelical speaker broadcasting under the direction of the Federal Council who, without fear or favor, preaches Christ and Him crucified. In a recent conference on radio broadcasting, held under the auspices of the Ohio State University, it was recommended that religious programs should be addressed to a cross-section of the public, to Protestants, Catholics, Jews, and non-believers, and not to members of any one faith. It was recommended that religious programs should not appeal for contributions, either directly or indirectly, for the support of the radio program itself, nor should it charge for sermons, pamphlets, or religious objects distributed through religious programs to be used by the sponsor as a means of raising funds.

Now there is some virtue in these attitudes, but the result of the execution of such a program will be the complete elimination of Protestant evangelical broadcasting. Under the present set-up, free time is given to the liberals alone. Gospel broadcasters must pay for their time. Access to free time on the radio chains is not possible, and there is a strong effort being made to hinder us from buying time to preach the Gospel.

Unfortunately, considerable radio racketeering is indulged in by evangelical preachers. They have raised large sums of money by means of radio broadcasts, handled it loosely, and given no accounting to anyone in financial matters. These men in their selfishness and carelessness are jeopardizing the whole evangelical radio program. The government is "catching up" with them and, I suspect, will not long permit them to operate and profit personally through radio broadcasts.

We should have in America a strong organization of evangelical broadcasters which will provide a "front" to deal with the government and properly present the fundamental broadcasters' case, in times of emergency. This organization will furnish also a clearing house for Gospel broadcasts and eliminate racketeers who are injuring all of us. Some of our so-called fundamentalists have gone to Washington, claiming that they officially represented fundamentalism, and have demanded certain privileges. I have been told upon good authority that these men have made the Federal Communications Commission angry, and they have said that they will not recognize factionism. However, they will recognize and must recognize accredited authority. We must awaken to the fact that we are rapidly approaching some form of totalitarianism in America and that rugged individualism in all forms and all places, at least for the duration, is out. We must surrender some of our independence for a solid interdependence and, trusting in God, we must stand against growing paganism in our land.

All disassociated groups are in danger. Politicians are careful, however, not to antagonize strongly united groups.

III. THERE ARE DANGERS TO OUR COUNTRY AND TO THE KINGDOM OF GOD IN OUR UNRELATED DIVISIONS

In evangelism lies the hope of a godly America. We cannot keep our liberties without godliness.

> Ill fares the land to hastening ills a prey,
> Where wealth accumulates, and men decay.

Modernism destroys foundations and provides a culture for the growth of the germs of all forms of evil. It destroys faith in the Bible, in Christ, in righteousness, in revivalism, and has given us the God-forgetting paganistic civilization which is so disastrous to every good thing in our land. Today, this same modernism would silence every voice raised in behalf of Christian patriotism, for many modernists have a greater interest in the outworking of some form of Marxism than in the salvation that comes through our Lord and Savior, Jesus Christ. The inroads of wild socialistic theories through the power of organized minorities in government are creating a cancerous condition in America. Not only is there surreptitious entrenching of radicals in high places in our governmental life, but a tendency is manifest even on the part of high officials to smear any who call attention to these cancerous adhesions to our body politic.

It is not boasting to declare that evangelical Christianity has the America of our fathers to save. While our army and navy fight the enemy without, we have the enemy at home to battle, and he is in some ways more dangerous than the enemy abroad. We unhesitatingly declare that evangelicals have the "keys of the kingdom." Millions of evangelical Christians, if they had a common voice and a common meeting place, would exercise under God an influence that would save American democracy.

The old slogan, "United we stand; divided we fall," is certainly applicable to the dangers of the fragmentized condition of evangelical Christianity in America.

NOTES

1. National Association of Evangelicals Executive Committee, *Evangelical Action!: A Report of the Organization of the National Association of Evangelicals for United Action*, (Boston: United Action Press, 1942). Public domain.
2. H. W. Evans, "The Klan of Tomorrow" (Atlanta: Knights of the Ku Klux Klan, 1924), 8–9.
3. "Mission and Work," *National Association of Evangelicals*, March 17, 2020, https://www.nae.net/about-nae/mission-and-work/.

CHAPTER NINE

"Segregation and the Kingdom of God"

Christianity Today

E. EARLE ELLIS

March 18, 1957[1]

Southern Baptist theologian and New Testament scholar Edgar Earle Ellis spent the majority of his academic career on the Southwestern Baptist Theological Seminary faculty in Fort Worth, Texas. He was well-published and well-regarded among his conservative Evangelical peers.

In the first year of Christianity Today, *however, Ellis was part of a cover story on the Evangelical response to the early years of the Civil Rights movement. The Montgomery Bus Boycott had ended three months earlier. And two months in the future, Billy Graham, a founder of* CT, *would irritate Christian segregationists by interrupting his New York City Crusade to preach at the American Baptist Convention with Martin Luther King—a deliberate choice to align with what white Southern Protestants deemed a revolutionary.[2] Before his New York crusade, the* Times *reported Graham as saying that King "[sets] an example of love" that Graham tries to emulate in his racially integrated meetings.[3]*

This was the rhetorical situation into which Ellis, a staunch and credentialed Southern Baptist, was speaking. Notice how he clearly maintains binaries—not only between the races, but also between North and South, between integrationists and segregationists, and between evangelicals and atheists. The divide is clear between the agents and counter-agents in his drama. How does he treat his argumentative adversary? What is the position of the African American citizen in his drama? How does either act?

In 2018, Christianity Today *editor Mark Galli stated editorial regrets over publishing Ellis' essay. He explained that "we were naïve about the ugly realities of segregation, and how little it was or could be realistically directed by a Christian conscience …. We were completely ignorant about the nature and stubbornness of structural injustice."*[4] *The bifurcation that Ellis insists upon Galli simply conflates under the pronoun "we." Is that enough to counter-state Ellis' apologia for racism defended with Christian tropes?*

Race relations are probably the most important problem agitating the Christian conscience today. Secular integrationists are calling upon the Church to speak to the problem—assuming that if it "spoke," it would call for the solution that the integrationists demand. As a matter of fact, the Church has spoken and is speaking, but it does not speak with one voice. The cleavage is particularly apparent if one avoids that un-Protestant confusion of the voice of the clergy with the "voice of the Church." Since the Supreme Court decision of 1954, the issue has been focused in terms of "segregation" versus "integration." Within this framework, Christian integrationists champion their position as "the Christian way" and dismiss the views of segregationists as naïve or prejudiced.

Most of the integrationist press treats the question as if all segregationist thinking stemmed from emotional, ignorant or ulterior motives. Religious periodicals, with some exceptions, tend to identify integration with Christianity and segregation with the forces of iniquity. This attitude is not just an oversimplification; it is a basic distortion of the issues. It identifies the principle of segregation with certain evils in segregation-in-practice. It illogically leapfrogs from the proposition, "Integration is concordant with Christian race relations," to the contention, "Integration is necessary for Christian race relations." Finally, it ignores the injustices present in integration-in-practice in the North and the evil implicit in a consistent integrationist philosophy.

A SOUTHERN POINT OF VIEW

Few Southerners—certainly few Christians—will defend in *toto* segregation-in-practice in the South. Too often the color line has been viewed as horizontal rather than vertical; unchristian white men—like unchristian men everywhere—have used their racial status to bully or to prey upon the weaker group; and the slogan "separate but equal" has preserved the separate and forgotten the equal. The greatest sin of Christian segregationists has not been their individual relationship with Negroes but their indifference to chronic injustices within the dual social system. In the forties, Virginius Dabney and a number of other Southerners organized to correct some of these injustices within the segregation formula. Dabney cites the reason for their failure (*American Magazine,* August, 1956): "There was no cooperation from influential segments of Southern society. The result of such indifference was the removal of the Negro capital from Atlanta to New York and the shifting of Negro leadership from Southern moderates to Northern radicals."

This is not the whole story, however. Raymond Moley has correctly identified the two salient facts in the segregated South over the past half-century—the great progress of the Negro and the great improvement in racial attitudes. Within the segregation pattern, the South has opened the door to the professions for the Negro, in some ways surpassing integrationist areas. In each of several Southern states, for example, there are as many Negro school teachers (receiving "equal pay" and in some areas a higher average pay) as in thirty-one Northern and Western states combined (cf. Dabney); segregated Meharry and Howard universities have provided more Negro doctors than all of the integrated institutions of the North. For several decades preceding the Supreme Court decision, inequities had declined and the business and professional strata of Negro society had increasingly developed. "In the South they have segregation," replied a Mississippi Negro to his surprised Northern college professor, "but Southerners are kinder to Negroes than Northerners are." Segregation does not necessitate bad race relations, nor does integration guarantee good ones. On the contrary, the very opposite often appears to be true.

It is sometimes asserted that segregation almost always is associated with domination of and discrimination against the weaker group. It would be more accurate, however, to say that whenever diverse groups have been associated under a political unit, whether on an integrated or a segregated basis, the tendency has been to discriminate against the weaker. This is true of some "integrated" minority groups in Europe today—a problem that finds a "segregation" solution in the political realm through racial, rather than merely geographical, representation in parliament. On the other hand, eastern Canada is an example of segregation equitably administered. The French and the English have separate schools and churches, move in their own social circles and maintain distinct cultural divisions in an attitude of mutual respect.

It is not unnatural that the Christian in the North should look askance upon segregation. He can see no good reason for it (the "melting pot" philosophy worked for the Poles and the Germans, why not for the Southerner and the Negro?); he weighs it in terms of individual discriminations, e.g., the inferior Negro school (a complaint passé in many areas) or the poorer Negro residential area; and he hears of it only in caricature. Emotional and sentimental factors are particularly strong where the problem can be solved by a slogan. It is no secret that the integration sentiment of most white Christians increases in direct proportion to their distance from the Negro as a group factor in society.

The integrationist, viewing the problem as one of "personal" exclusion, overlooks or denies the relevancy of treating it as a group relationship. Christians in the South have a different reality to face: There is *de facto* a biracial society with vast numbers of each group; cultural, sociological and psychological differences between the races are considerable. (Only a naïve appraisal can reduce the problem to one of "skin color.") Freedom of association, in the eyes of the South, is a liberty applicable to group as well as individual relationships. The white South desires— and holds it to be a right—to preserve its European racial and cultural heritage; this cannot be done if integration is enforced in social institutions, e.g., the schools. Intermarriage, whether in the 2nd generation or the 10th, is a question which, in Alistair Cooke's phrase, "only the intellectual, the superficial and the foreigner far from the dilemma can afford to pooh-pooh" (*Manchester Guardian Weekly*, May 24, 1956). The soothsayer may confidently predict that this will not happen, or publicize as the "scientific" view (as though scientists were agreed on the matter) that racial differences are merely physical and environmental. The essential point is that the people who must live in the situation are convinced, for reasons sufficient for them, that integration will be destructive of their society, ultimately an evil rather than a good. (Compare H. R. Sass, "Mixed Schools and Mixed Blood," *The Atlantic*, Nov., 1956.) And they are confident that, where the white and black races live together in considerable numbers, the concept of a dual society applying a principle of segregation in varying degrees according to the exigencies of particular situations will, when directed by a Christian conscience, provide the more equitable and harmonious relationship.

The master-servant relationship is passing in the South, and some modus vivendi is desperately needed to replace it. Segregation has the potential to develop into a partnership of mutual respect; this partnership can never arise from a judicial force bill which is intolerable to one of the groups. Southerners often wonder whether integrationists are as interested in good race relations as in forcing a particular kind of race relations. The unfortunate fact is that ardent Christian integrationists, however conscientious, are one cause of the worsening race relations in the South today. Their moral superiority complex, their caricature of the segregationist as an unchristian bigot and their pious confession of the sins of people in other sections of the country have not been wholly edifying.

Segregation in America is, and should be, a fence not a wall, a division with many openings. In former years in the South, the writer occasionally visited colored churches and enjoyed their fellowship in an atmosphere of Christian love; they on occasion visited his. At that time segregation was the norm, recognized and approved by both groups; yet it was no bar to friendship or fellowship in many areas. Then came the integrationist, a self-righteous harbinger of a "new world a-comin'," pounding his pulpit drum and condemning all opposition to Gehenna. The outlines of his new world have come: and what is the cause of the growing resentment, fear, animosity and discord? Why, the segregationist, of course!

ACROSS THE OHIO

Whatever appeal integration has for Southern Negroes, it has been produced by the current identification of everything bad with segregation and everything good with integration. Even to the more sophisticated outside the South, the word still casts a spell, but some of its luster no doubt has faded. They came north to the promised land, but they crossed the river to find it wasn't Jordan at all but only the Ohio. In the North Negroes are integrated—at the bottom. There are exceptions, of course, but by and large integration-in-practice is full of discriminations: A Negro student sometimes cannot fulfill his requirements because no integrated school will accept him for student teaching. In Negro sections business and professional services are largely in the hands of whites. There is no "separate but equal" formula to equalize facilities between "white" New Trier and Chicago's "black" south-side schools.

If the 90-year integration experiment in the North had produced a just and amicable relationship, it might be more attractive to the South. Actually, integration has most signally failed in just those areas which most nearly approximate—in population ratio—the Southern scene. The integrationist "blockbuster" approach is exemplified by Trumbull Park (Chicago) where Negroes were assigned to a white housing project. The result has been riot, race hatred and a 24-hour police guard for more than a year. In nearby Gary, Indiana, Andrew Means, a Negro contractor, using a segregationist approach, has built six Negro suburban-type communities. Race relations are good. Nevertheless, integrationists encounter a mental block at the suggestion that segregation has merit as a pattern for living in a multiracial society.

The Southerner can understand the sentimentalist, but the inconsistency of most integrationists is harder to comprehend. In the integrationist North, papers often censor local racial unrest (to prevent riot), then editorialize about immoral segregation in the South. When teaching Sunday School in Chicago's "black" south side, the writer failed to encounter any homes of Christian integrationists. They live in "white" suburbs, send their children to "white" schools, and then travel through Negro areas to their editorial offices, professions and businesses where they expatiate against segregation. Sometimes they favor admitting a Negro to their suburb if he is the "right kind" of Negro. A Christian friend of the writer, quite integration-conscious, mentioned having had Negro dinner guests. "Of course," he added, "they were clean and educated—no one like Isaac (our janitor)." Is this the fulfillment of New Testament ethics?

The point is not that the integrationist would defend integration-in-practice in the North. But in condemning the segregationist's failure to achieve a "separate and equal" society, the integrationist fails to realize the implication of his own failure to achieve a "mixed and equal" society. This failure hardly recommends integration as "the solution" to racial discrimination and animosity—a goal that both groups seek. If Southern Christian leaders can do no better than to follow the integrationist approach of their brothers to the North, the future is less than bright.

AND THE KINGDOM OF GOD

Both integrationists and segregationists are extremely eager to quote God as on their side. However, the Scriptures most frequently used, the "curse of Ham" argument in Genesis and the "one blood" argument in Acts, are irrelevant. The New Testament does indeed picture all Christians as being united. In Christ there is neither Jew nor Greek, male nor female, free nor slave, rich nor poor, educated nor ignorant, clean nor dirty, black nor white (cf. Gal. 3:28; Col. 3:11). But in New Testament Christianity this is a unity in diversity, a unity which transcends differences and works within them, but never a unity which ignores or denies differences or necessarily seeks to erase them. The servant is no less a servant, the master no less a master; the rich no less rich, and the poor no less poor. The New Testament ethic is not "we are the same, there is no difference; we are equal, therefore I love you" but rather "we are not the same, we are not equal in many ways; but I love you and desire your good." The Gospel was not primarily to change the pattern of society, but to bring to bear new motives and new attitudes within the pattern. It is true that Christianity effected changes in the pattern, but its approach was totally different from the integrationist's philosophy today.

Integration as a moral imperative has its roots in a secular view of the Kingdom of God in which the Kingdom is identified with the church and ultimately with the society of this world, and is to be brought in by social reforms. For the New Testament, however, whatever its manifestation within the Christian community is, the Kingdom of God is never to be identified with or find its consummation in a this-world society.... Even within the church, the differences between individuals and/or groups are not done away. Paul and Barnabas came to the conclusion that in certain circumstances their best unity lay in separation (Acts 15:36–46). Jewish and Gentile Christians differed in many practices, e.g., the observance of the Sabbath and other Old Testament laws (Rom. 14:5, 6; Acts 18:18; 21:23 ff), differences that ultimately resulted in "ecclesiastical" separation. Not only does the Apostle not view these differences as sinful, but he rather insists on the right of the groups to continue in them (Gal. 2:5; Rom. 14). In other words, the unity of Christians does not necessarily mean a physical "togetherness" or organizational conformity; the Kingdom in the church does not negate the church's relation to the social customs of the world and of the churches: The same Paul who said that there was neither male nor female in Christ also instructed women to be silent in church (cf. 1 Cor. 11:4; 14:34).

The creed of consistent integrationist Christians could be summed up in the phrase, "the right to belong"; and their heresy, "the refusal to belong." In their minds, "togetherness" is a good, exclusiveness an evil. God—whatever else he is— is certainly "democratic"; segregation is "undemocratic" and therefore immoral.

Only when one applies the philosophy of integration consistently—thankfully most integrationists are not consistent—can he see its full implications. In Christ, there is no rich nor poor; therefore, says the economic integrationist, we must integrate society through Christian socialism to eliminate evil class distinctions. It is wrong, cries the political integrationist, to discriminate against a man because of "an accident of birth"—birth in a foreign country; world government and world citizenship are the answers to this wrong. The ecclesiastical integrationist intones: denominations are evil per se, they divide us; we must fulfill Christ's prayer "that they may be one" by uniting in the "coming great church." Segregation is discrimination, concludes the racial integrationist, and "de-segregation" is its cure.

The argument for racial integration and the use of governmental force to implement it is a part of a pattern that is very evident in other areas of life. (And how often the voices in the argument vaguely remind one of voices heard at other times, on other issues.) It is a bad argument. Christian communism does not yield a good economic relationship; the "one church" organization does not give true Christian unity; cultural leveling does not produce a common bond of friendship; integration does not alleviate racial animosity and injustice. Further, it is an argument that is ethically anemic: in the name of equality it destroys the liberty of individuals and groups to live and develop in associations of their own preference; in the name of unity it points with undeviating insistence toward authoritarianism and conformity, eschewing the inherent sin root in human society with its inevitable consequence: power corrupts and total power corrupts totally.

If the Kingdom of God as a monolithic homogeneous structure is the goal of Christian ethics—if national, economic, cultural, racial, ecclesiastical distinctions are to be abolished as "immoral," then the integrationist argument is sound. But if the Kingdom of God is seen as intersecting—and yet above—a this-world framework, compatible with—and yet superseding—the many and varied distinctions in this present age; then segregation is, in principle, an equally valid answer. And in practice it is much more compatible with liberty. Christian integrationists are patently sincere in the path they are forging, but the road signs along that path sometimes remind one more of Aldous Huxley's *Brave New World* than of the New Testament's Kingdom of God.

NOTES

1. E. Earle Ellis, "Segregation and the Kingdom of God," *Christianity Today*, March 18, 1957. Reprinted by permission of the publisher.
2. "Baptists Open Philadelphia Session," *Plain Speaker* (Hazelton, Pennsylvania), May 29, 1957, 2.
3. Stanley Rowland, Jr. "As Billy Graham Sees His Role," *New York Times*, April 21, 1957, 193.
4. Mark Galli, "Where We Got It Wrong," *Christianity Today*, January 1, 2018, 27–28.

CHAPTER TEN

"The Cross and the Sickle"

BILLY JAMES HARGIS

Los Angeles, California
May, 1966[1]

As the American hot war against the Nazis morphed into the American Cold War against the more ambiguous Communists, American ministers adapted their rhetoric too. The conservative Evangelical ministers were their loud and incendiary selves. Billy James Hargis is an exemplar of Richard Hofstadter's conclusion that the "constant struggle against world communism" gave the revivalist preacher "a new lease on life."[2]

Hargis was ordained as a Disciples of Christ minister at age seventeen, studied for one year at Ozark Bible College, and then began to pastor a church in Sapulpa, Oklahoma. He eventually finished degrees at two degree-mills, Pikes Peak Bible Seminary and Burton College.

He started the Christian Crusade *in 1950 and his school American Christian College in 1971—both to counter-balance what he perceived as left-wing ideology in American culture and higher education. Hargis was forced to step down from the leadership of that school in 1974 when five students came forward as victims of his sexual predation.* Time Magazine *stated that the first two victims to report on Hargis' assaults were on their honeymoon—each confessing to the other that they were victims and each discovering that the same minister who married them also assaulted them. The Vice President of the American Christian College, David Noebel heard all the reports including Hargis' justification: "Noebel was told that Hargis justified his homosexual acts by citing the*

Old Testament friendship between David and Jonathan and threatened to blacklist the youths for life if they talked."[3]

"The Cross and the Sickle" was Hargis' stump speech. He would deliver it several times, adapting to specific locales and recent events. In this speech you see the intersection of all the knee-jerk issues he claimed were connected to Communism: racial integration, denominational ecumenism, gay rights, and anti-Vietnam sentiment. Notice how his dramatistic antagonist is like Billy Sunday's and Bob Jones'—lurid and exciting, sinning in the most titillating ways. Those aligned with Hargis simply and passively stand.[4] *What's the role of the arts for Hargis? Why are they his antagonists? What happens if you remove the specific term for an antagonist—"Marxists" or "National Council of Churches"—and replace it with a scapegoat in our current public sphere? What happens to the larger drama? Does it still hang together?*

Now, ladies and gentlemen I believe that the National Council of Churches is an instrument of Satan. I don't think it's any good today, and I don't think it ever will be any good. It's not good for freedom. It's not good for religious orthodoxy. It's not good for spiritual traditions. It's not good for our political or patriotic traditions. The National Council of Churches is an alien group. It is a Marxist group. Politically, it is an agnostic group. Theologically, it is out of step with the Bible. It's out of step with Church history. The National Council of Churches does not speak for 40 million Protestants in the United States, and they lie when they say that they do.....

Every problem in the United States today—race agitation, immorality, and even a socialistic-political revolution—is due directly to both active leadership of the National Council of Churches or its failure to declare itself in defense of Christian traditions. I contend that every problem that confronts us internally today is the making of the National Council of Churches, perhaps more than any other organization in this country.

Now first of all, race agitation. I said that they were responsible for race agitation and that they are. The National Council of Churches, as I said changed its name from Federal Council that in 1950, they have long been agitating minority races in the United States for what I believe to be not spiritual reasons, but political reasons. The National Council of Churches published this book which is called *The Negro American: A Reading List.*[5] And if you haven't seen this book which proves that they are race agitators, as I said, and the role that they play in racial agitation, I ask you to write to me, Our Christian Crusade, Tulsa, Oklahoma, enclose one dollar, and we'll send you four copies of it: one to keep and three to distribute.

We have reproduced the National Council of Churches reading list. This book put out by the National Council of Churches indicts themselves. Now listen to what they say in the introduction. They are telling preachers that they are to stock these books that they recommend. They're to stock them in their church libraries and not to be satisfied there. They're to get these books in the school libraries so that young people in America will understand the "Negro American." Now, they say one, "these books are safe to recommend to children especially in junior high school and elementary grades."They're going after the kids young which, of course, is the old philosophy of Lenin. Lenin said, "Give me a boy or a girl until he is seven, and he will be a Marxist forever.". . .

Now, who are the authors that they recommend? Well ladies and gentlemen, let's just take a view. First of all, they recommend Herbert Aptheker. Herbert Aptheker, as you know, is the editor of the Communist monthly magazine in the United States. His daughter is the girlfriend of Mario Savio, who created the disturbance at Berkeley, California, if you want to know some little intimate facts.[6] . . .

Let's go to the second author. The second author the National Council of Churches recommends is W.E.B. DuBois. Who is DuBois? Well, ladies and gentlemen, the NAACP, and I know a lot of fine white people and a lot of fine Negro people that have been completely misled by the NAACP.

I have tried to tell my Negro friends that the NAACP is not your friend. The NAACP is trying to use the American Negro to advance some liberal white men's political biases, and that's all it is. For instance, you can't ignore the fact there were seven founders of the NAACP, only one of them was a negro. The only one that was a Negro was W.E.B DuBois, who was a Communist. He admitted he was a Communist. He said he was a member of the Communist Party. Can you believe a man when he says he's a Communist? I think so. W.E.B DuBois, a member of the Communist Party, was one of the seven founders of the NAACP.[7] The NAACP will not allow a Negro president. They've never had a Negro president ....It's a one-family, white socialistic-political action program that has fooled a lot of good Negroes and white people alike.

Now ladies and gentlemen, W.E.B. DuBois was a red. He's married a woman by the name of Shirley Graham who's still alive. DuBois died, thank God, two years ago, but Shirley Graham's still alive. I mean that his wife still works for the *Communist Worker*. Now, W.E.B. DuBois is one of the authors recommended by the National Council ....

Let's go to the next name. The next name is Langston Hughes. Langston Hughes is the favorite author on this subject of the National Council because they recommend one, two, three, four, five, six, seven, eight, nine of his books. They want you to put nine books by Langston Hughes in your church library. By the way, Langston Hughes, who as you know, has been under fire for years because of his pro-communism, has now gone back to work for the NAACP. You see, it's no longer unpopular for a Communist to work for a liberal group.[8] Your Hollywood Ten, your producers and writers that were outlawed because of Communism ....

This Langston Hughes that we're talking about is best known for a blasphemous poem called, "Goodbye Christ," and this is typical of some of his writing.[9]

… This is the author most recommended in the *Negro American* by the National Council of Churches.

It would not be a difficult thing for me to stand up here and show you how the National Council of Churches was involved in the St. Augustine riots. How that attorneys that are on the paid staff of the National Council of Churches appeared in St. Augustine even before the revolution broke out, and as soon as the so-called civil riders were arrested they were bailed out and defended by the National Council of Churches.[10]… This again is the role of the National Council of Churches in the racial agitation field.

Well, let's go to the second point I said: they were also responsible for this current wave of immorality. But let me review just a little, and this is all things that just happened.

Here's the *New York Times* for Sunday January 17th this year. The headline says "Minister Defines True Obscenity."[11] Now, the minister's name is Reverend Howard Moody. He's pastor of a Protestant Church affiliated with the NCC. He's often quoted in the NCC circle. He's very popular as a lecturer. Pastor of the Judson Memorial Church, 55 Washington Square, South of New York City. Let me quote the *New York Times*:

> "Vulgar speech and often spoken, but seldom printed, four-letter words are not immoral or blasphemous according to the New York Baptist minister." the Reverend Howard Moody. Reverend Moody "maintains today that vulgar and body language may well be objected to, on the basis of … social manners," but it is not a moral case. "It is hardly justifiable to make a moral or a theological case against raw language, as the Church has tended to do."

He goes on to say that his position—his crusade against forbidding vulgar speech and all-spoken four-letter words in public circles and in church circles, his crusade against any such prohibition has the support of—"well-known theologians Reinhold Niebuhr and John C. Bennett."…

This, my friends, is the perversion not only of religion, but the perversion of morals and integrity that unfortunately is not only being permitted by religious leaders, but in some instance, is actually being encouraged. Now, let me give an example of that. This just happened, by the way. In fact, it happened just a few months back in December 21st, to be exact, just prior to Christmas, last year for the Christmas sermon on the campus of Baltimore's Goucher College. Now this is a girls' school. This is a school for girls and they hire a chaplain and, of course, these chaplains always have to be in agreement with the National Council of Churches because the National Council and their associates control these sensitive positions as chaplains of these universities. The chaplain of Baltimore's Goucher College is the Reverend Dr. Frederic C. Wood, Jr. For his Christmas sermon, before an audience filled with girl-students at this select school, he decided to preach on premarital sexual relations. I actually have a script of his message, and I'll read you a portion of it, "Sex is good, sex is fun, it's also funny. Premarital intercourse is not bad or dirty. Indeed, it can be very beautiful. Sex is natural. We ought not take sex so seriously. We all ought to relax, and stop feeling guilty about our sexual activities, thoughts, and desires. Sex is interpersonal. It involves two people. Free love is not detrimental." And on, and on, and on.[12]

Now, this was the chaplain, the Protestant chaplain, of the Goucher Girl College in Baltimore, Maryland, and his pre-Christmas message is telling these young ladies that they need not feel a sin-guilt or guilt complex about premarital sex relations. And you asked me why the United States is going nuts?...

Now, let's add to that something that happened right here in your own territory. I'm holding now a photostat copy of the *San Francisco Chronicle* for January 18th, for January 3rd, and for December the 7th. This has to do with these Methodist and Episcopal clergymen in San Francisco who are preaching homosexual practices as legitimate and not a sin among the youth of the San Francisco Bay area.

First of all, let me quote from the January 18th *Chronicle*:

> A prominent Methodist pastor, the Reverend John V. Moore made an appeal to the members of his congregation yesterday to devote some of their time to a dialogue between overt homosexuals and lesbians. This appeal was made during a spirited seminar in the Glide Memorial Methodist Church following a sermon by Mr. Moore on the needs to integrate homosexuals into the churches in the Bay Area.

> Nearly 150 men and women remained after the service and spent an hour wrestling with such questions as, one: What is normal in bed? And second: What is a seduction? When is a seduction antisocial?

> Moore was helped in this speech welcoming homosexuals into this Methodist Church by an attorney in the congregation, with the name of Evander Smith. And Evander Smith added some things to the sermon by the Reverend Mr. Moore, he said that queers or homosexuals were particularly averse to molesting little children.

Well, I'm sure that this is not in keeping with the police records of Los Angeles County. For years, and years, and years the FBI and Hoover and the police authorities have told us that a homosexual is the most likely breed of people to molest children. But, according to a Methodist preacher in San Francisco, all of this information put out by crime enforcement officials is wrong, and one of the best ways that you can prevent child molesting I suppose, by his reasoning, is everybody be a homosexual....

So, there you have it my friends. I believe that the Church of Jesus Christ ought to set an example of righteousness and virtuous living. And when a minister participates in fields like this, this man is not fit to be a minister of the gospel of Jesus Christ. I would point out to you that none of these preachers urging integration of the church with homosexuals, or urging the church to change its mind concerning sodomy—none of these ministers voted for [Barry] Goldwater. They're all in acceptable churches, the liberal variety associated with the National Council of Churches.

Without exception, the National Council of Churches is back to the socialistic-political revolution. We'll get into South Vietnam now, and you must hear this. I don't know if you read it or not: 75 officers of the National Council of Churches called on Secretary of Defense McNamara and demanded that we get out of South Vietnam. They claimed they spoke for 40 million Protestants which, of course, is a lie ....

Now, ladies and gentlemen, if the National Council of Churches speaks for you in the statement [on Vietnam] then you ought to stay in your church. But if the National Council of Churches does not speak for you in this instance, you ought to keep your money out of that organization and put it in some movement like Christian Crusade that's trying to save this country and carry on an anti-communist cause....

But, you remember this, my beloved friends, at the same time you have a national cause like Christian Crusade. And unless you support these national causes your local causes don't have a China-man's chance for survival. Because, if they ever wipe us out on the top level, then they get next to you. And how could you survive with just a handful of people in a little town?

We are buffeted. We are serving as buffers for the whole cause of Christ. They're hitting at us, and I don't mind it if the people will stand with us and enable us to carry on our activities in spite of all the tremendously well-financed opposition.

Well, my friends, I want to tell you, before there was a Christian crusade today that has chapters all over America, hundreds of thousands of friends, millions of listeners ... before we had this success, there was a Gethsemane when we suffered, and when everyone turned against us. Even members of our own family would have nothing to do with us because they couldn't understand. And I know these ministers who are for the first time in their lives militantly opposing Communism. I know what they're going to go through, if they're not already going through it. So pray for these young men who for the first time are taking a stand, because Satan throws everything he has at these men....

Is it any wonder that in the Book of Revelation, when you read of the coming world government, the Bible points out that that world government will have a world church at its side. The Bible says ultimately every nation will lose its identity, and Satan will dwell over the face of the earth as a world dictator. Satan, incarnate in the person of the anti-Christ, and at his side will be the world church, world amalgamation of religions, pagan and Christian. My friends, you can go on as you've been going on, put your money in new cars and finer homes, better businesses, nicer fur coats, and you're going to see this country topple around you just like that house built on sand. I tell you, my friends, my biggest discouragement is when I see God's people failing to accept a responsible role in this fight to preserve Christian freedom in the world. It's up to the Church of Jesus Christ....

Everything I've said for 20 years on radio was true. I said Communism was our enemy, now the Communists are killing your sons in South Vietnam. I said there was Communism on college campuses, now the liberals are admitting that there's Communism on college campuses, including Berkeley. Everything we have said was true. They ridiculed us. They held us up in contempt. They questioned our motive. Even the administrations moved against us, and we had to go out with tin-cups and beg people to give us a dime or a quarter to save their kids and their kids. And then when I got a few dollars to buy a few minutes of radio time, they questioned my motives and called me a patron for profit. How much can one human being take? I've taken twenty years of ridicule and contempt. But bless God. I'd rather die fighting Communism than ever live under Communism.

NOTES

1. Billy James Hargis held a three-day conference called, "God and Country Forum" at the Hacienda Hotel in Los Angeles on May 20–22, 1966. Major General Edwin A. Walker was also a featured speaker. "Evangelist will Hold Conference, *Los Angeles Times*, May 8, 1966, 26. Billy James Harris, "The Cross and the Sickle," Fayetteville: University of Arkansas, 1952. Reprinted by permission of the archives.
2. Richard Hofstadter, *Anti-Intellectualism in American Life*. (New York: Knopf Doubleday, 1963), 146.
3. "The Sins of Billy James," *Time*, February 16, 1976, 52.
4. For a longer dramatistic analysis of the rhetorical *code duello* in conservative political speeches, see Camille Lewis, "'Remove Not the Ancient Landmarks': Making the Confederate Distortions of Religion Apparent," *Was Blind But Now I See: Rhetoric, Race, Religion, and the Charleston Shootings*, Landham, MD: Lexington Books, 2019.
5. *The Negro American: A Reading List* (New York: National Council of Churches, 1957), https://files.eric.ed.gov/fulltext/ED019355.pdf.
6. Bettina Fay Aptheker, born September 13, 1944, is a Distinguished Professor of Feminist Studies at UC Santa Cruz.
7. DuBois was never a member of the Communist Party. David Levering Lewis, DuBois' biographer, explained that fact as well as the intense criticism he received from the Communist Party, who described him as a "class enemy." David Levering Lewis, *W. E. B. Du Bois, 1868–1919: Biography of a Race* (New York: Owl Books, 1993) 513–517.
8. Langston Hughes never joined the Communist Party because he felt its rules were too rigid. He testified to this in 1953. "Testimony of Helen Goldfrank (Kay) and Langston Hughes," *Senate Permanent Subcommittee on Investigations of the Committee on Government Operations*, March 24, 1953, https://www.k-state.edu/english/nelp/childlit/radical/McCarthy_Kay_ Hughes.html.
9. Arnold Rampersad, David Ernest Roessel, eds. *The Collected Poems of Langston Hughes* (New York: Vintage Books, 1995) 166–167.

10. For details, see Dan R. Warren, *If it Takes All Summer: Martin Luther King, the KKK, and States' Rights in St. Augustine, 1964* (Tuscaloosa, University of Alabama Press, 2008).

11. "Minister Defines 'True Obscenity: Moody Calls Dirtiest Word 'N-----' Uttered by Bigot," *New York Times*, January 17, 1965, 48.

12. Wood preached this sermon on October 26, 1964 in the Haebler Memorial Chapel at Goucher College in Towson, Maryland. Hargis seems to be quoting from the *New York Times* December coverage of the October sermon. "Minister Defends Lenient Sex View: Says Goucher College Talk Did Not Use Promiscuity," *New York Times*, December 7, 1964, 42. Frederic C. Wood, "Sex within the Created Order," *Theology Today*, 22, no. 3 (October 1965): 394–401. doi:10.1177/004057366502200308.

CHAPTER ELEVEN

"Black Manifesto"

JAMES FORMAN

May 1969[1]

After growing up in abject poverty in Mississippi and struggling through systemic racism and injustice in his young adult life, James Forman graduated from Chicago's Roosevelt University in 1957. He organized with the Student Nonviolent Coordinating Committee (SNCC) and was a frequent critic of Martin Luther King. He saw King's methods as too authoritarian and discouraging to "ordinary people" since "interjecting the Messiah complex" would make "people … feel that only a particular individual could save them and would not move on their own to fight racism and exploitation."[2] Despite the differences between the two men, King and Forman together marched on the Alabama capitol on March 16, 1965.[3]

Forman left the leadership of SNCC, and within five years the organization's influence diminished. However, in Detroit in April 1969, Forman participated in the Black Economic Development Conference where the group adopted this "Black Manifesto"— the first call for reparations.[4] Forman took that document and presented it to the National Council of Churches on May 2.[5] And then during a Sunday morning communion service two days later at Manhattan's Riverside Church, Forman marched down the aisle and waited for the choir to finish, "When Morning Gilds the Skies." As the pastor began his sermon, Forman read the Manifesto aloud. All but 500 people left their seats, some weeping.[6] A week later Forman returned to stand during Pastor Ernest Campbell's sermon whispering, "peace, peace" occasionally.[7] Forman would later receive a Master's in

African and Afro-American studies in 1980 and his Ph.D. in 1982 from the Union of Experimental Colleges and Universities.[8]

What's the dominant element in Forman's rhetorical drama? Whom does he craft as the primary actor? When he stands before a church of mainline liberal Protestants reading this statement, how does he cast himself in the drama? Is he different than an athlete "taking a knee"? How do current arguments for reparations resemble Forman's initial volley?

We the black people assembled in Detroit, Michigan for the National Black Economic Development Conference are fully aware that we have been forced to come together because racist white America has exploited our resources, our minds, our bodies, our labor. For centuries we have been forced to live as colonized people inside the United States, victimized by the most vicious, racist system in the world. We have helped to build the most industrial country in the world.

We are therefore demanding of the white Christian churches and Jewish synagogues which are part and parcel of the system of capitalism, that they begin to pay reparations to black people in this country. We are demanding $500,000,000 from the Christian white churches and the Jewish synagogues. This total comes to $15 per n-----. This is a low estimate for we maintain there are probably more than 30,000,000 black people in this country. $15 a n----- is not a large sum of money, and we know that the churches and synagogues have a tremendous wealth and its membership, white America, has profited and still exploits black people. We are also not unaware that the exploitation of colored peoples around the world is aided and abetted by the white Christian churches and synagogues. This demand for $500,000,000 is not an idle resolution or empty words. Fifteen dollars for every black brother and sister in the United States is only a beginning of the reparations due us as people who have been exploited and degraded, brutalized, killed and persecuted. Underneath all of this exploitation, the racism of this country has produced a psychological effect upon us that we are beginning to shake off. We are no longer afraid to demand our full rights as a people in this decadent society.

We are demanding $500,000,000 to be spent in the following way:

1. We call for the establishment of a Southern land bank to help our brothers and sisters who have to leave their land because of racist pressure for people who want to establish cooperative farms, but who have no funds. We have seen too many farmers evicted from their homes because they have dared to defy the white racism of this country. We need money for land. We must fight for massive sums of money for this Southern Land Bank. We call for $200,000,000 to implement this program.

2. We call for the establishment of four major publishing and printing industries in the United States to be funded with ten million dollars each. These publishing houses are to be located in Detroit, Atlanta, Los Angeles, and New York. They will help to generate capital for further cooperative

investments in the black community, provide jobs and an alternative to the white-dominated and controlled printing field.

3. We call for the establishment of four of the most advanced scientific and futuristic audio-visual network to be located in Detroit, Chicago, Cleveland and Washington, D.C. These TV networks will provide an alternative to the racist propaganda that fills the current television networks. Each of these TV networks will be funded by ten million dollars each.

4. We call for a research skills center which will provide research on the problems of black people. This center must be funded with no less than 30 million dollars.

5. We call for the establishment of a training center for the teaching of skills in community organization, photography, movie making, television making and repair, radio building and repair and all other skills needed in communication. This training center shall be funded with no less than ten million dollars.

6. We recognize the role of the National Welfare Rights Organization, and we intend to work with them. We call for ten million dollars to assist in the organization of welfare recipients. We want to organize the welfare workers in this country so that they may demand more money from the government and better administration of the welfare system of this country.

7. We call for $20,000,000 to establish a National Black Labor Strike and Defense Fund. This is necessary for the protection of black workers and their families who are fighting racist working conditions in this country.

8. We call for the establishment of the International Black Appeal. (IBA) This International Black Appeal will be funded with no less than $20,000,000. The IBA is charged with producing more capital for the establishment of cooperative businesses in the United States and in Africa, our Motherland. The International Back Appeal is one of the most important demands that we are making for we know that it can generate and raise funds throughout the United States and help our African brothers. The IBA is charged with three functions and shall be headed by James Forman:

   a) Raising money for the program of the National Black Economic Development Conference.

   b) The development of cooperatives in African countries and support of African Liberation movements.

   c) Establishment of a Black Anti-Defamation League which will protect our African image.

9. We call for the establishment of a Black University to be funded with $230,000,000 to be located in the South. Negotiations are presently under way with a Southern University.

10. We demand that IFCO allocate all unused funds in the planning budget to implement the demands of this conference.

In order to win our demands, we are aware that we will have to have massive support, therefore:

1. We call upon all black people throughout the United States to consider themselves as members of the National Black Economic Development Conference and to act in unity to help force the racist white Christian churches and Jewish synagogues to implement these demands.

2. We call upon all the concerned black people across the country to contact black workers, black women, black students and the black unemployed, community groups, welfare organizations, teachers' organizations, church leaders and organizations explaining how these demands are vital to the black community of the U.S. pressure by whatever means necessary should be applied to the white power structure of the racist white Christian churches and Jewish synagogues. All black people should act boldly in confronting our white oppressors and demanding this modest reparation of $15 per black man.

3. Delegates and members of the National Black Economic Development Conference are urged to call press conferences in the cities and to attempt to get as many black organizations as possible to support the demands of the conference. The quick use of the press in the local areas will heighten the tension, and these demands must be attempted to be won in a short period of time, although we are prepared for protracted and long-range struggle.

4. We call for the total disruption of selected church sponsored agencies operating anywhere in the U.S. and the world. Black workers, black women, black students, and the black unemployed are encouraged to seize the offices, telephones, and printing apparatus of all church sponsored agencies and to hold these in trusteeship until our demands are met.

5. We call upon all delegates and members of the National Black Economic Development Conference to stage sit-in demonstrations at selected black and white churches. This is not to be interpreted as a continuation of the sit-in movement of the early sixties, but we know that active confrontation inside white churches is possible and will strengthen the possibility of meeting our demands. Such confrontation can take the form of reading the Black Manifesto instead of a sermon or passing it out to church members. The principle of self-defense should be applied if attacked.

6. On May 4, 1969 or a date thereafter, depending upon local conditions, we call upon black people to commence the disruption of the racist churches and synagogues throughout the United States.

7. We call upon IFCO to serve as a central staff to coordinate the mandate of the conference and to reproduce and distribute in mass literature, leaflets, news items, press releases and other material.

8. We call upon all delegates to find within the white community those forces which will work under the leadership of blacks to implement these demands by whatever means necessary. By taking such actions, white Americans will demonstrate concretely that they are willing to fight the white skin privilege and the white supremacy and racism which has forced us as black people to make these demands.

9. We call upon all white Christians and Jews to practice patience, tolerance, understanding, and nonviolence as they have encouraged, advised and demanded that we as black people should do throughout our entire enforced slavery in the United States. The true test of their faith and belief in the Cross and the words of the prophets will certainly be put to a test as we seek legitimate and extremely modest reparations for our role in developing the industrial base of the Western world through our slave labor. But we are no longer slaves; we are men and women, proud of our African heritage, determined to have our dignity.

10. We are so proud of our African heritage and realize concretely that our struggle is not only to make revolution in the United States, but to protect our brothers and sisters in Africa and to help them rid themselves of racism, capitalism, and imperialism by whatever means necessary, including armed struggle. We are and must be willing to fight the defamation of our African image wherever it rears its ugly head. We are therefore charging the Steering Committee to create a Black Anti-Defamation League to be funded by money raised from the International Black Appeal.

11. We fully recognize that revolution in the United States and Africa, our Motherland, is more than a one-dimensional operation. It will require the total integration of the political, economic, and military components; and therefore, we call upon all our brothers and sisters who have acquired training and expertise in the fields of engineering, electronics, research, community organization, physics, biology, chemistry, mathematics, medicine, military science and warfare to assist the National Black Economic Development Conference in the implementation of its program.

12. To implement these demands we must have a fearless leadership. We must have a leadership which is willing to battle the church establishment to implement these demands. To win our demands we will have to declare war on the white Christian churches and synagogues and this means we may have to fight the total government structure of this country. Let no one here think that these demands will be met by our mere stating them. For the sake of the churches and synagogues, we hope that they have the wisdom to understand that these demands are modest and reasonable. But if the white Christians and Jews are not willing to meet our demands through peace and good will, then we declare war and we are prepared to fight by

whatever means necessary. We are, therefore, proposing the election of the following Steering Committee:

- Lucious Walker
- Renny Freeman
- Luke Tripp
- Howard Fuller
- James Forman
- John Watson
- Dan Aldridge
- John Williams
- Ken Cockrel
- Chuck Wooten
- Fannie Lou Hamer
- Julian Bond
- Mark Comfort
- Earl Allen
- Robert Browne
- Vincent Harding
- Mike Hamlin
- Len Holt
- Peter Bernard
- Michael Wright
- Muhammed Kenyatta
- Mel Jackson
- Howard Moore
- Harold Holmes

Brothers and sisters, we no longer are shuffling our feet and scratching our heads. We are tall, black, and proud.

And we say to the white Christian churches and Jewish synagogues, to the government of this country and to all the white racist imperialist: there is only one thing left that you can do to further degrade black people, and that is to kill us. But we have been dying too long for this country. We have died in every war. We are dying in Vietnam today fighting the wrong enemy.

The new black man wants to live and to live means that we must not become static or merely believe in self-defense. We must boldly go out and attack the white Western world at its power centers. The white Christian churches are another form of government in this country, and they are used by the government of this country to exploit the people of Latin America, Asia and Africa, but the day is soon coming to an end. Therefore, brothers and sisters, the demands we make upon the white Christian churches and the Jewish synagogues are small demands. They represent

$15 per black person in these United States. We can legitimately demand this from the church power structure. We must demand more from the United States Government.

But to win our demands from the church which is linked up with the United States Government, we must not forget that it will ultimately be by force and power that we will win.

We are not threatening the churches. We are saying that we know the churches came with the military might of the colonizers and have been sustained by the military might of the colonizers. Hence, if the churches in colonial territories were established by military might, we know deep within our hearts that we must be prepared to use force to get our demands. We are not saying that this is the road we want to take. It is not, but let us be very clear that we are not opposed to force, and we are not opposed to violence. We were captured in Africa by violence. We were kept in bondage and political servitude and forced to work as slaves by the military machinery and the Christian church working hand in hand.

We recognize that in issuing this manifesto we must prepare for a long-range educational campaign in all communities of this country, but we know that the Christian churches have contributed to our oppression in white America. We do not intend to abuse our black brothers and sisters in black churches who have uncritically accepted Christianity. We want them to understand how the racist white Christian church with its hypocritical declarations and doctrines of brotherhood has abused our trust and faith. An attack on the religious beliefs of black people is not our major objective, even though we know that we were not Christians when we were brought to this country, but that Christianity was used to help enslave us. Our objective in issuing this Manifesto is to force the racist white Christian Church to begin the payment of reparations which are due to all black people, not only by the Church but also by private business and the U.S. government. We see this focus on the Christian Church as an effort around which all black people can unite.

Our demands are negotiable, but they cannot be minimized, they can only be increased and the Church is asked to come up with larger sums of money than we are asking. Our slogans are:

ALL ROADS MUST LEAD TO REVOLUTION
UNITE WITH WHOMEVER YOU CAN UNITE
NEUTRALIZE WHEREVER POSSIBLE
FIGHT OUR ENEMIES RELENTLESSLY
VICTORY TO THE PEOPLE
LIFE AND GOOD HEALTH TO MANKIND
RESISTANCE TO DOMINATION BY THE WHITE CHRISTIAN CHURCHES AND THE JEWISH
    SYNAGOGUES
REVOLUTIONARY BLACK POWER
WE SHALL WIN WITHOUT A DOUBT

NOTES

1. James Forman, "Black Manifesto," (New York City: Episcopal Church Archives, 1969). Reprinted by permission of James Forman, Jr.

2. James Forman, *The Making of Black Revolutionaries* (Seattle: University of Washington Press, 200) 255.

3. Roy Reed, "Police Rout 600 in Montgomery; 8 Marchers Hurt," *New York Times*, March 17, 1965, 1.

4. Ronald J. Stephens, "Black Manifesto," *Encyclopedia of Black Studies* (Newbury Park, California: Sage Publications, 2005), 129–30.

5. "Church Group Gets a Black Manifesto," *New York Times*, May 3, 1969, 14.

6. Emanuel Perlmutter, "Black Militant Halts Service at Riverside Church," *New York Times*, May 5, 1969.

7. George Dugan, "Forman Stands Silent, Through Riverside Church Sermon," *New York Times*, May 12, 1969, 37.

8. Joe Holley, "Civil Rights Leader James Forman Dies," *Washington Post*, January 11, 2005.

CHAPTER TWELVE

"Christian Manifesto"

CARL MCINTIRE

July 20, 1969[1]

Carl Curtis McIntire, Jr. was livid when he heard about James Forman's "Black Mani-
festo." By 1969, McIntire had already left the Presbyterian Church USA and the Ortho-
dox Presbyterian Church over the Protestant doctrine of eschatology (McIntire was a
dispensationalist) and alcohol consumption (he was a teetotaler). As a result, he formed
his own Bible Presbyterian denomination—a group founded to be more politically active
as well as more strictly pious. McIntire started his own newsletter, The Christian Bea-
con *and his own radio show,* Twentieth-Century Reformation Hour. *He also founded*
two church councils, the American Council of Christian Churches and the International
Council of Christian Churches—both as alternatives to the liberal-leaning National
Council of Churches and the World Council of Churches. Suffice it to say, McIntire loved
to incite trouble and then leave the room.

With Forman getting media and ecclesiastical attention, McIntire could not leave
well enough alone. So he constructed his own "Christian Manifesto," demanding that
mainline liberal Protestant churches allow him to read the statement aloud in their
churches. He first asked Abington Presbyterian Church after Muhammed Kenyatta had
read the "Black Manifesto" there on July 14, 1969.[2] The church refused.

But McIntire's irritation paid off a month later when he got to read his "Christian
Manifesto" at the same Riverside Church Forman had interrupted. Calling Forman
a "voice of hell" and proof of "the Communist participation in the internal life of the
church in the United States of America," McIntire attempted to speak over the organ

music at the front of the church, but Pastor Campbell quietly interrupted him. Campbell explained that he would be breaking the law if he continued, so McIntire acquiesced and read the statement on the church steps outside. After finishing, he taped a copy of the 13-page document to the entrance of the church, autographed a few Bibles, and left.[3]

McIntire created this statement as a counter-statement "to offset and be a counter-part to the Black Manifesto." How does McIntire's impersonation of Forman's statement change the perception of either? In presenting the fundamentalist Christian as equally enslaved as any American of color, how does McIntire change the ongoing conversation? Forman had allies and contributors. McIntire only had himself and a few aides. Who is the primary actor, then, in his drama?

TO THE MODERN CHRISTIAN CHURCHES IN THE ECUMENICAL BODIES

Introduction

TOTAL SUBMISSION TO THE WORD OF GOD, WHICH IS THE SCRIPTURES OF THE OLD AND NEW TESTAMENTS, IS THE ONLY SOLUTION TO ALL THE PROBLEMS FACING MANKIND.

Brothers and Sisters:

The Prophet Amos said it is an "evil time," and Christians who stand by the Bible throughout the entire world are burning with righteous indignation. They are suffering persecution and affliction at the hands of apostates, modernists, and unbelievers who call themselves Christians and who by their political maneuverings have captured major denominations and are using these resources, which run into the multiplied billions of dollars, not for the advancement of the historic Christian faith and the carrying out of the Great Commission of Jesus Christ, but for the purpose of building a one-world church, a superworld-state.

There can be no separation of the problems—economic, political, cultural—from the commands of God as set forth in the Ten Commandments given to Moses on Mount Sinai as he led the Children of Israel from Egyptian bondage.

There are still people, millions of them, who are clinging to the rhetoric of Christianity, including its hymnology and poetry, who no longer believe the Scriptures.

We must separate ourselves from many who call themselves Christian leaders who go around the country promoting socialism, Communism, calling for the recognition of Red China, the establishment of normal relations with Communist Cuba, and the immediate unilateral withdrawal from Vietnam.

Ironically, some of the most militant apostates, who call themselves ecumenical, are pretending to be expositors of the Bible and believers in freedom. Jesus Christ described such as "wolves" "in sheep's clothing." The Bible calls them "blind guides," "hypocrites," of whom Jesus said they could not "escape the damnation of hell" (Matt. 23).

In the United States the charges of "racist," "imperialist government" are the shibboleths used to destroy a responsible capitalism and the American way of life.

We speak for Bible-believing Christians. The return of the Jews to Palestine represents a fulfillment of prophecies in anticipation of the return of Jesus Christ bodily to this earth to stand on the Mount of Olives. We are concerned about all the propaganda that turns blacks against whites, poor against rich, and in the name of the Gospel promotes the class struggle. Duped into believing that peaceful coexistence as heard from Moscow is the road to peace, church leaders are participating in ecumenical gatherings where the Communists have their spokesmen honored as Christian leaders.

We as Bible-believing Christians must be concerned about the salvation of the lost in every part of the world and must repudiate all racial strife, violence, and revolution. We repudiate the Black Manifesto, which calls for a society where the total means of production are taken from the rich and placed in the hands of the State for the so-called welfare of all people. There are those who have been bewitched by the cry of racism, those who are opposed to the benevolence of industry, those who are attacking the police, those who are repudiating law and order and calling for guerilla warfare in the streets. The ideology that they profess must be seen to be born of atheism, Marxism, socialism, Communism. The exploitation of the church for revolution, the infiltration of religion for the destruction of religion, and the use of such terms as "the kingdom of God" and "making all things new" to represent such destructive forces must be rejected by all who have respect for decency and God. Revolution must be met by reformation. The spiritual, moral, and political conditions can be corrected only by a confession of sin, repentance toward God, and faith toward the Lord Jesus Christ.

The age long conflict between God and Satan, Christ and antichrist, righteousness and wickedness, freedom and tyranny summons all Christians to battle the forces of darkness and slavery. We maintain that we have the Reformation right to do this, and as the church was reformed and the blessings of liberty followed the Sixteenth-Century Reformation, a Twentieth-Century Reformation is the imperative of the present hour. Wherever the Black Manifesto is presented in churches, assemblies, office buildings, and conference headquarters, this Christian Manifesto must also be presented.

The Black Manifesto is the voice of hell, not the fruit of the Spirit. It is the evidence of Communist participation in the internal life of the churches in the United States of America. It is the fruit of the social gospel. It will destroy the United States.

The Christian people affiliated with the International Council of Christian Churches in the United States of America and throughout the world are fully aware of the unbelief and apostasy that has gained control of the major denominations in the United States, whose voice is that of the National Council of Churches, and, for so many now, of Janes Forman, heralded as a modern-day prophet. Those who have held the fundamental doctrines of the Christian faith have been persecuted, exploited, deposed, driven from their properties, and all the resources rightfully theirs taken from them to be used in the development of the ecumenical church. The recognition of the validity of reparations by the churches in the National Council of Churches and by the World Council of Churches leads us to present the demands for reparations to those who have suffered at the hands of the liberals during the twentieth century. These reparations are due not only in the United States but in Canada, Great Britain, Europe, Scandinavia, India, Pakistan, Korea, and other lands wherever the ecumenical missions have taken possession of properties and are using them against the faithful church leaders who would preserve the Christian faith.

We, therefore, demand of the churches which have accepted and tolerate in their fellowship inclusivism, permissivism, the new morality, existentialism, and the "God is dead" theologians, that they immediately make full restitution and reparation, returning to the Bible-believing people throughout the world that which is spiritually, morally, and historically theirs. To take properties and monies and institutions established by Bible-believing people and to use them to build socialism, destroy capitalism, and banish the true Christian faith constitutes a crime against the law of God upon which Heaven itself shall pronounce the judgment.

Ruin, crime, murder, rape, the spirit of lawlessness, and riot are the direct result of the failure of modern churches. Their abandonment of the Gospel that saves souls and regenerates by the Holy Ghost, and their deliberate appeal to Statism constitutes an offense against every law-abiding Christian and Jew. The reparations now demanded are not figurative or ethereal. They represent the actual shift of rightful ownership. The recent Supreme Court decision deciding that, because of separation of Church and State, the courts must leave in the hands of the churches such matters as fidelity to doctrine, faith, discipline, and the properties involved, has given to the liberal majorities a power to crush fundamental minorities who morally are entitled to funds given to support the things which they believe and which the apostates would destroy. The court decision makes imperative this Christian Manifesto and its appeal to justice and conscience.

In the United States, all of the historic Christian shrines that have upon them quotations from the King James Version of the Bible; all of the historic churches that go back to the founding fathers, whose cemeteries are filled with the remains of those who died believing in a bodily resurrection, which is the faith of the fathers and the faith of the churches of the Reformation today; all of the buildings, institutions, endowments, colleges, universities, and hospitals that were established before the rise of liberalism and the unbelief of the Fosdicks, the Buttricks, the

Oxnams, the Bennetts, the Van Dusens, the Pikes, the Altizers, the Barths, the Coffins, and others—all rightfully belong to the Bible believers, the successors to those who believed the Bible in their day. The use of Christian resources and heritage to destroy Christianity involves an immorality that is as great as any committed in church history.

The International Council of Christian Churches, raised up of God, believing the Bible to be his infallible and holy Word, rejecting the ecumenical apostasy, repudiating the new creeds including the Confession of 1967, now demands that all of these resources be subject to the demands of reparation and that such be turned over to the fundamental church bodies comprising this Council and others that have been raised up as a result of unbelief. A colossal crime has been committed by those forces that have usurped the authority of Scripture and have taken the resources of Christianity to build a Babylon church.

In view, therefore, of the fact that the principle of reparations is now being accepted as valid in ecumenical circles, we hereby demand of the churches in the United States affiliated with the National Council of Churches the sum of three billion dollars. This is a low estimate in view of all that has been acquired from the hands of those who have believed the faith once delivered unto the saints. This figure is almost infinitesimal when compared to the budgets of the nations and the cost of wars of the nations. We are not unaware of the exploitation of our Christian brethren of all colors—black, brown, red, yellow, white—who have been victimized by vain, empty words.

Stimulating all of this exploitation has been a rejection of the Gospel, a repudiation of the Christ of the Bible, a use of chat which was rightfully His to promote the spirit of antichrist. We are no longer afraid to demand our rights under God. The affirmations of love, tolerance, brotherhood, humanity, made by the liberals must now be tested alongside of the demands of the Black Manifesto for money. We are demanding that the money be spent in the following ways:

1. We call for one billion dollars to be used for the sole purpose of evangelizing the nations with the message of the blood of Christ and 500 million dollars for the erection of hospitals in which the Gospel of Christ be presented with the healing knowledge of modern science; these funds to be contributed through the Commission on Evangelism of the International Council of Christian Churches to the 140 denominations who are presently preaching this message. The use of this money for the spiritual blessing of mankind will immediately alter the economic, the social, and the political needs of the world and will bring the blessings that God has promised, "For your heavenly Father knoweth that ye have need of all these things" (Matt. 6:32)—food, raiment. The church must attend to its primary task of obeying the Great Commission (Matt. 28:19–20).

2. The call for the establishment of 18 major publishing and printing centers in the United States, Brazil, Argentina, London, Amsterdam, Beirut, Lagos, Nairobi, Johannesburg, Lahore, Madras, Singapore, Auckland, Adelaide, Hong Kong, Taipei, Seoul, Tokyo, These centers will provide the literature for the Reformation and the information to deliver the nations from the Communist deceptions and totalitarian powers. For this 30 million dollars is asked.

3. We call for the establishment of theological seminaries and Christian institutions of higher learning that will defend the Christian faith and will "promote on every continent … an educational system for all ages which shall be free from the blight of rationalism and in which the Bible shall be basic, to the end that education may again become the handmaid of the Church rather than a foe to the whole Christian conception of God and the world." For this 200 million dollars is allocated, plus an additional 50 million dollars for miscellaneous.

4. We call for the establishment of four of the most advanced scientific and futuristic audio-visual networks to be located in Detroit, Chicago, Cleveland, and Washington, D.C. These TV networks will offset the networks established by the Black Manifesto and will be an alternative to their false racist propaganda. Total funds for the financing to be 250 million dollars, including purchase and operation.

5. We call for research skills centers that will provide research on the problems of all people, of all colors and of all races, with a view to assisting them to help themselves, including black capitalism, and not to be dependent upon the powers of government for their existence. This center must be funded with no less than 50 million dollars.

6. We call for the establishment of training centers for the development of Christian skills and competence in photography, television, repairs, radio, building. This training center shall be funded with no less than 10 million dollars, and will counter the Black Manifesto.

7. We call for the establishment of six powerful international short-wave transmitters which will offset similar radio ministries presently operating in Africa, the Philippines, and Communist countries. These will disseminate the Gospel behind the Iron Curtain and provide information presently being withheld to the people of the world, and will "advocate steadfastly the Christian mode of life in society at large in the hope that we may be able to do something to retard the progress of atheistic and pagan ideologies under any name, of loose morality and of godlessness which have become such alarming threats to the Christian method of life in our times" (Constitution of ICCC, Art, VII, 11). For this we request 100 million dollars.

8. We call for the support of International Christian Relief, to be funded by no less than 500 million dollars and to bring in the name of Jesus Christ the nurture of love and human kindness.

9. We call for funds in the amount of ten million dollars to support the National and Regional Councils of Churches in every nation and region where possible for the purpose of maintaining the liberties and the rights of Bible-believing Christians. This includes the establishment of the world headquarters of the International Council of Christian Churches in Geneva, Switzerland, to represent the glories of the faith of those who proclaimed, "After darkness light." Reparations must include the transfer of Calvin's historic church to the Twentieth-Century Reformers that it may no longer be desecrated by ecumenical unbelief and used as a mockery to Calvin and Luther, Knox and Zwingli, and those others whose statues are on the Reformation Monument of that city.

10. We call for 300 million dollars to be used especially for and by the Negroes, and ask that this fund be provided only to fundamental Negro churches separated from the National Council of Churches and the World Council of Churches. The fund is to be used to inform all the Negroes who have been misled by false accusations of racism and the nature of Christian brotherhood and to persuade the Negroes in the United States and the world that their first need is Jesus Christ as presented in His Gospel and that the Bible is the Book of their freedom. The hope of the world is not the Democratic Party and politically inspired material aid programs, which, when exhausted, will leave a vacuum of despair and rebellion. In Jesus Christ there is neither Jew nor Greek, neither bond nor free, neither black nor white, but all are one and this unity will bring respect for our God and His laws.

11. We include in these demands for reparations the transfer of keys and titles of institutions, colleges, and seminaries from the hands of the modernists who have occupied them on the basis of the "winner take all" philosophy of the modernists to the control of Bible-believing churches which have come into existence in the last 75 years to continue the true witness of the founders.

Princeton Theological Seminary, Princeton, N.J., was established by Presbyterians who believed the Westminster Confession of Faith. Its leadership has now produced the Confession of 1967. This institution must be turned over to the Bible Presbyterians.

Drew University, Methodist, located in Madison, New Jersey, represents the citadel of Methodist unbelief. It should be turned into the hands of former Methodist Protestants, the Bible Protestants.

Colgate-Rochester Divinity School, New York, with its library and buildings, properly belongs to the General Association of Regular Baptist Churches and should be delivered to them.

Southern Methodist University, Dallas, Texas, should be turned over to the Congregational Methodists.

Emory University, Atlanta, Ga., the product of Methodism in the South, which preached the Gospel of John Wesley, should have all of its properties and facilities turned over to the Southern Methodists.

In order to win these demands we are aware that we must have the massive support of all Christians in all churches and in all lands.

1. We call therefore upon all Bible-believing people throughout the United States and throughout the world to unite in prayer, fellowship, and cooperation to the end that the enemies of Christ and the forces of tyranny may meet their challenge by the Word of God.

2. We call upon all concerned with the apostasy across the country to demand that prayer and Bible reading be returned to the public schools of the United States and that the name of God be acknowledge and honored in our national life and that righteousness become the policy of our Government in dealing with ail governments.

3. We call for a complete exposure and repudiation of Communism in all fields of their sinister work, the winning of the war in Vietnam, the liberation of Cuba, and the exposure and defeat of Communism in the Western Hemisphere.

4. We call for a complete reappraisal of education, its materialistic, atheistic foundation, and the return of education to the people. All areas of national life where socialism is moving in with its destruction of initiative, personality, thrift, and responsibility must be challenged and rejected by Christian America.

5. We call for the maintenance of law and order; respect for the police; free, respectful, open debate; and the end to violence as a weapon of "democratic" procedure.

6. We call upon all clergy associated with the International Council of Christian Churches to challenge the Black Manifesto wherever it is presented and to request immediately the presentation of this Christian Manifesto, and that wherever the Black Manifesto is read the Christian Manifesto shall also be read.

7. We call for a complete repudiation of the National Council of Churches, a separation from it, and the support of churches that are not ashamed of the Gospel of Jesus Christ and of the persecutions that have come upon those

who have been defrocked and driven from their churches because of loyalty to Jesus Christ.

8. We call for Christians throughout the world to remember each other in prayer and to support one another in understanding, to believe the words of the prophets, and to confront the enemies of Christ with confidence—"Resist the devil, and he will flee from you" (Jas. 4:7). We are proud of our American heritage, the Bill of Rights, the Constitution of the United States, the Statue of Liberty, the American Flag, and we call upon all to resist the present revolutionary forces as they manifest themselves in the churches, the schools, the political parties, and any aspect of national life, and to resist the forces that are using racism, hate, the class struggle, war, riot, and armed rebellion.

9. We call for a fearless leadership that puts its faith and trust in Jesus Christ. We praise and commend the brethren of Pakistan where 85 percent of the Christians in the last one and one-half years have renounced the ecumenical movement and have preserved Christianity.

10. We call upon all Bible-believing churches to dedicate themselves to the purposes of this Christian Manifesto with the faith that God is able in these last days to enable such a witness to be given before the Second Coming of Jesus Christ and His deliverance of the Church, His body and Bride, from the power of death.

11. We call upon Christians to act in the spirit of the prophets and the apostles, counting their lives not dear to themselves and manifesting the spirit of the hymn of the Reformation, "A Mighty Fortress Is Our God"…

Christians have the Hope of the world who is Jesus Christ. They possess the Gospel which is, "Christ died for our sins according to the scriptures; and that he *was* buried, and that he rose again the third day according to the scriptures" (1 Cor. 15:3, 4); and which testifies: "The word is nigh thee, even in thy mouth, and in thy heart: that is, the word of faith, which we preach; that if thou shalt confess with thy mouth the Lord Jesus, and shalt believe in thine heart that God hath raised him from the dead, thou shalt be saved. For with the heart man believeth unto righteousness; and with the mouth confession is made unto salvation. For the scripture saith, Whosoever believeth on him shall not be ashamed, For there is no difference between the Jew and the Greek: for the same Lord over all is rich unto all that call upon him. For whosoever shall call upon the name of the Lord shall be saved" (Rom. 10:8–13).

We call for salvation and reformation, not revolution and slavery. The Christian Manifesto challenges the Black Manifesto and it calls upon all who have been redeemed to stand up, be counted, endure afflictions, put on "the whole armour of God … and having done all, to stand."

NOTES

1. Carl McIntire, "Christian Manifesto," New York, 1969. Reprinted by permission of C. T. McIntire.
2. "McInitire Talk Vetoed by Abington Church," *Philadelphia Inquirer*, July 16, 1969, 8.
3. "Church 'Reparations' Demanded for Fundamentalists," *New York Times*, September 15, 1969, 1.

PART 5

Redeeming America from Its Original Sin

By the 1990s and 2000s, the struggles of the Civil Rights movement faded for most of white America. For a narrow group of white Protestants, however, the conflicts of the Civil War were as near as ever. And as we move into the twenty-first century, the Woman Problem and the Negro Problem and the Red Problem splintered into sexual identities, gun violence, and public memory. The President of Greenville, South Carolina's Museum to the Confederacy, Terry Rude represents that narrow group of Protestants who sound as much like Henry Grady and John Roach Straton as ever. In Springfield, Missouri, Pastor Phil Snider counter-states—and even directly cites—that narrow group with his advocacy for gay rights. And in this climate, two politicians contest white rule. President Barack Obama calls America to grace, and New Orleans Mayor Mitch Landrieu calls his city to repentance.

CHAPTER THIRTEEN

"Southern Manhood"

TERRY RUDE

April 1991[1]

After growing up in California, Terry Lee Rude earned a Masters of Divinity in 1976 and a Ph.D. in Old Testament Theology in 1979, both from Bob Jones University in Greenville, South Carolina. He taught religion at his alma mater from 1972 through 2001. Since arriving in South Carolina, Rude has cultivated a strong affinity for the Confederacy, and in his role as a chaplain for the Sons of the Confederate Veterans, he has been a vocal apologist for the Southern Lost Cause since 1990.

Rude frequently preaches this sermon, "Southern Manhood." In his public state-ments over the last several decades, Rude himself embodies the persona he is describing. His source material is straight from Lost Cause mythology and, thus, is very typical of white supremacist rhetoric over the last century. What is the drama at work? How would you characterize Rude's hero of the Southern man? How would you describe his antagonist? What actions do both his protagonist and antagonist perform? How does Rude's persona of the Southern man compare with Bob Jones's persona of the Modern Woman in 1924? How does Rude counter-state the Northern liberals and academics like Ken Burns and General U. S. Grant? And we cannot ignore the silent participants in Rude's drama. How does he describe them?

Thank you, Brother Wilkins, my brother in the faith, my brother in the South.[2]

Abram Poindexter was a young man who commanded a company, Company K of the 46th Virginia regiment when the Northerners blew the great crater in the area of Petersburg, Virginia. This young man had a father who was a reverend. This young man was an ethical young man. A young man who was a gifted young man, wanted to be a teacher, and was president of the Talladega Academy in Alabama, but a young man who couldn't stay out of the War.

On that day, July 30, 1864—when the crater was blown and bodies were flying and a massive hole was broken into the Confederate ranks there, and the Yanks began to pour in like flood waters through a hole in a damn—Poindexter's company was almost devastated and all of the other officers had been taken from the field or wounded. Poindexter said to his men, "Boys, we must hold this position or die in our places, for the salvation of the town depends on the enemy not carrying these works." Very shortly after that another officer rode in the vicinity and saw these handful of men standing fast, and this officer said to them, "What are you doing? Where's your officer? Why are you here?" And they said, "There's our captain." They pointed to Abram's body. He'd been killed since he gave that command. They said, "our captain commanded us to fight to the death, to hold this ground and serve, and we aim to do it."

John Broadus years later conducted the funeral of Abram Poindexter's dad, and he told this story, relating how one of the men who had survived passed on the good word about this man's son to him. Conducting that funeral he told this story, and Broadus when he told the story he said this, "Truly that was a captain, and truly those were men." Truly those were men.[3]

My purpose this morning in this first talk is to share with you Confederate manhood. I think as we look overall, the masses of men that took part in that war over 125 years ago, our conscience obligates us to say, "truly those were men."

Now what can we learn of those men?

First of all, the Confederate manhood that they represented could boast some of the best intellects our country has ever produced. Now I'm not going to go back to the period before the War and share with you how many presidents have been Southerners and all of those things. But let me just share this with you. Robert Lewis Dabney: Seminary professor, Union Theological Seminary, [graduated from] Hampden-Sydney before the war, later went to Richmond. In those days [it was] a good, solid seminary, holding up the Word of God. This man was Stonewall Jackson's Chief of Staff during the Shenandoah Valley campaign.

The Jacksons knew the Dabneys, had stayed with them, when in April of '62, Dabney was being sought by Jackson to be the Chief of Staff. [He said,] "I don't know what I think about the military," and he rode on out to the area where Jackson was in the Swift Run Gap in the Shenandoah Valley to argue that he could not become the officer. And Jackson's reply was, as he made this very intellectual case that he couldn't be the officer, Jackson said, "Nonsense. Rest today. You don't have to start today. Study the articles of war today and begin tomorrow."

Dabney spent all day long devouring the articles of war. Here's a civilian, who knew nothing about the army at all, and the next day Dabney walked out of the headquarters a commissioned major—the Chief of Staff of Jackson's staff. Well, Colonel Grigsby of the 26th Virginia didn't take to that much. He was an ungodly man, and he made some kind of a mockery and said, "I concluded that old Jack must be a fatalist sure enough, because he put an Ironside Presbyterian parson as the Chief of Staff." And then Grigsby made some kind of mockery that at least he was relieved because he could clearly see that Jackson wasn't omniscient, and the implication was that he had made a great mistake. R. G. Tanner published in 1976 in his book *Stonewall in the Valley,* concluded this: "Dabney ignored the jokes and dug into the articles of war, a man of boundless intelligence. He proved himself quickly even to Grigsby."[4] And here was a man who was so gifted in character and gifted in his mind that he could be a commanding leader in just a night's study of a book, a book that would take most of us months and months and months merely to read, let alone to master.

I mentioned John Broadus. Broadus was a professor at the Baptist seminary in 1859 in Greenville, South Carolina where I'm from.[5] Nothing less than a building there, but the heritage of Broadus' remains. There's a street named after Broadus. One man wrote after the war about Broadus: "he rose to the very forefront of biblical scholars, writers, preachers, and has a reputation second to none on this continent."[6] When I came to seminary, the very first book recommended to me was a commentary on Matthew's Gospel published in the 1880s by John Broadus. Broadus was such a dynamic and elegant teacher and such a scholar of the Greek and English New Testament, that we today in 1991 still use his book on the preparation and delivery of such sermons in our ministerial program. It is that good. There has been nothing that has risen to that point since the day of Broadus.

These were intellectual men. These were men of character. These were Southern men. These were men who, in the classroom and also on the battlefield, had the character of young Poindexter....

And the first thing I want to acknowledge here is these men were patriots: fervent patriotism, an incredible patriotism. We know little of it today. We do nothing of it before the Gulf War here just in past weeks. A little spark has been lit in our country. It will soon go out. I'm sure it will soon go out. The liberals and the orientation of liberalism will see to that. But these men were patriots. These men loved God, or those that didn't love God respected God. But they learned and were taught in their homes to love their country. Patriots ....

I was drafted during the Vietnam era, and I served my country in that day I didn't go to 'Nam. I did my fighting on the computer here in the states. I was glad for that until I had my boys grow up and say, "Dad, you mean you didn't fight? Oh, Dad." But in those days, many a man burnt his draft card. And if you dared to burn the flag of this country, they are unworthy of this soil, they are unworthy of our constitution, they are unworthy of our land. And only in recent times did those who risked and spent their lives get recognized in that conflict.

But that wasn't the case in that war over 125 years ago. Those Southern boys had been taught at their hearts and at their tables and at their mom's knees to love Dixie and to love the South and to respect their state. My friend, we need that manhood. We need that today. We need that patriotism that marked that manhood.

But then there's another thing that I will share with you in regard to that manhood. Not only did some of the best intellects fight for the South, not only is there a characteristic record of their manhood, but they were indeed, as we have said and noted, by and large a people under Christian influence.

Let me read to you what the premiere Southern historian Douglas Freeman says in his preface to *Lee's Lieutenants* to clarify something of the nature of the era in which he wrote. This is written by this man in 1942. It had been seven decades essentially since the War between the States had ended. Freeman writes, "those war letters and diaries of the 1860s exhibit as marked a difference from the present-day thought on religion as perhaps ever has been wrought in any seven decades."[7] Did you get the point? The difference between his day in 1942 and what had happened in the war, which now was 125 years ago, he said is as radical or marked difference in religious shifting and thinking ever could have happened or probably ever did happen in any seven decades. I think he was right.

He went on to say, "Many of those men kept religion in the same sanctuary of the heart with patriotism and love of home. Acceptance of traditional Christianity was almost universal." This is a secular historian saying this. I doubt that Freeman was a truly born again Christian. I doubt it much. I hope I'm wrong, but I doubt it from his writings. "Mild and reverent deism was viewed with horror. Doubt was damnation. Agnosticism was service to anti-Christ. What was believed was professed. The example of Lee and Jackson in attributing victory to God was duplicated in 1,000 letters." In the 1940s, people were beginning to snicker to conservatism that characterized the old south and caused these southern states to be called the Bible belt. They don't snicker today; they openly laugh and mock ….

Now, I share with you what the Public Broadcasting System just said a few months ago of Jackson. "Jackson was a religious fanatic. Jackson was a pious, blue-eyed killer reluctant on Sundays even to read a letter from his wife whom he called 'Little Dove' but utterly untroubled by the likelihood of death." Did you get the mockery? Did you feel a sting? Did it pain your inner being? A religious kook and a nut who was reluctant to read a letter from his wife on Sunday. The series goes on to say, "Some thought him mad. He used no pepper because he said it made his left leg ache. He believed that only by keeping one hand in the air could he stop himself from going out of valor. He preferred to stand rather than to sit for fear of putting his internal organs out of alignment, and he sucked constantly on lemons even in the heat of battle. Others worried that his religious servitude would cloud his judgement. His command, Jackson believed, was the army of the living God."…[8]

My friend, the world doesn't care for Stonewall Jackson, I'll tell you why. One, he's a Southerner. Two, he was a godly man with an incontestably clear statement of faith in the Scripture as the very Word of God and personal faith and the person and work of Jesus Christ. But I say, this Southern manhood illustrated leadership, and at the very heart of that leadership were Christian principles.… People will rail and mock and ridicule one of the greatest Americans who ever lived. That PBS series gave some credibility to Lee and did some acknowledging of Lee, I'm thankful for that, was shocked about that. But we are so far away from respect for Scripture, and respect from Christian norms and values that it could gush forth as mockery of Jackson, and few things have I ever heard said negative about it people will say, "Oh, wasn't it a wonderful series?" That's like a guy who's sunk in a sewer, sticking his head out and says, "isn't this a wonderful atmosphere?"

I say to you, ladies and gentleman, we propose a choice: a choice to believe the truth, to believe the facts, to believe the records that were written and left behind by those who knew these men and those who were there, or to believe the Public Broadcasting System and to believe the modern historians. Modern historians as a norm are no friend of the south, no friend of Lee and Jackson, no friend of the Christian manhood of which I speak now. What are we going to do about that? I think we need to be devoted to duty as these men were devoted to duty ….

Duty is the sublimest word in the English language. I come from Bob Jones University. The chancellor's [grand]dad, Alex Jones, was wounded on the 20th of September 1863 at Chickamauga. He was wounded and limped all of his life on his right leg. Those who wrote the record about it said he often would say he's as proud of that wound as he is of any of his family members. They often kidded him about how he was prouder of that wound than he was of his own kids. That was 1863, 20 years later in 1883, Bob Jones Sr. who founded the university where I minister was born, and Alex Jones was wondering what to name him. And he noticed it's been 20 years exactly after that time. He got to thinking about when he got his wound his buddy, Robert Reynolds, stuck back in the trench with him to help him when the order came to move on. He had a great debt of love for Reynolds because of his personal care and all. And so he decided to name Bob Jones Sr., Robert Reynolds Davis Jones. The Robert Reynolds after his companion in the trench at Chickamauga, the Davis after Jefferson Davis, the unique president of the Confederacy. And so it was that he was named that, he made tapes in the 1950s (he was an old man by then), and the radio station WMUU plays those tapes, and I try to listen to those frequently in the morning. There was a period last year, which was an interesting year because it was the termination of the 125th anniversary of the war. And almost every tape that I listened to for a number of mornings he would cite this from Lee, "Duty is the sublimest word in the English language." He would often change it to, "duty is the noblest word in the English language." And here is this preacher citing these old Southern principles, and

I share this with you to point out that when I began to study carefully Southern heritage and Southern manhood, I saw a lot of the things that I only knew to be sayings from Bob Jones, Sr.[9]

Very often the School has been criticized of idolizing the man. Now this man never sought his own glory, but I realized this man was simply passing on what his dad, Alex who had fought in an Alabama regiment at Chickamauga and had been wounded, passed on to him. It's called manhood, Southern manhood, devotion to duty, devotion to truth, the truth in the Word of God, devotion to patriotism, devotion to that which is proper and right. Devotion to that which the founding fathers of this nation held up before their people. But I would like finally to share with you that this Confederate manhood produced not only all of those things, but fearless fighters, fearless warriors ….

Should I hold up before my two sons and my daughter Grant, who all but ate cigars in time of battle? Should I hold up the language of Sherman and Grant and the others? Should I hold up their character? Or should I hold up the character of Jackson? The character of a man who loved whiskey, but never drank it, never drank it because he liked it so well and was afraid he couldn't keep control over it. Should I hold up the character of a man who disdained profanity in his hearings and often chided his commanders when they would use even words like "hell." Should I hold up the character of a Jeb Stewart who vowed to his mother that he would never drink and, even when he was mortally wounded and dying, refused to take the spirits (I guess it was whiskey) until finally the pain got so desperate and the doctor kept urging him to do that. A Lee who didn't drink, should I hold up that kind of character or should I hold up a drunken Grant and the cigar-smoking Grant and a cigar-smoking Sherman? Now you have to do in your own conscience what you feel is right. And I think that if a person walks with God, then he'll perhaps cut off things that he might indulge in ….

Not long ago, the *Greenville News* published a little article on how one of [John Brown] Gordon's descendants out in California met a colored man named Gordon, the descendant of one of Gordon's slaves. It was a great reunion. The most fascinating thing about that is that this black man who's about my age (he looked to be in his forties. I'm 44), this black man said that his great granddaddy had told him that his people served Gordon just as much in the 1880s as they served Gordon before the war. Now, of course, the article didn't say why, but I'll tell you why. Gordon was a Christian man and loved his blacks. He treated them right, and so it turns out that this man was able to muster up in his staff incredible, fearless manhood.[10]

Finally, let's turn our attention to the symbol that represents all this character, all this patriotism, all this manhood. The symbol that represents these things. It's that flag right there, that flag …. A few years ago Georgia was trying to design a stamp to commemorate the statehood of Georgia. And they had a lot of interesting memorabilia there, and off to the side was a photograph of Robert E. Lee. And the government rejected that artist's proposal because it had a portrait of a slave owner. Too bad they didn't know Lee freed his slaves before the war, but Grant didn't finally free all of his slaves until Lincoln alleged Emancipation Proclamation in January of 1863. Too bad those people had not been taught at the fireside by their moms and dads and their knees that Lee was one of the most noble leaders the South ever had. Too bad those men had not been taught what truth and justice ought to have taught them. Too bad those men had not been taught what that flag symbolizes.... They loved those flags and will love them forever as the mementos of the unparalleled struggle. They cherish those flags because those battle flags represent the consecration and courage, not only of Lee's army but of all the Southern armies, and because those flags symbolize the bloodshed and the glory of nearly a thousand battles." Those flags symbolize the bloodshed and the glory of nearly a thousand battles.[11] ...

I say to you, that flag needs to fly. That flag does not stand for slavery. That flag does not stand for racism. That flag does not stand for the mockery it receives in 1991. That flag stands for the manhood I tried to portray before you today. That flag stands for the blood and the glory, the Southern blood, and the Southern glory of almost a thousand battles. That flag needs to fly.

Let us pray. Lord, we thank thee for the banner of love that sent thine only begotten Son to the cross to die for us. Your flag over us is love and truth, justice. But then Lord we thank thee for these men who knew you and walked with you and sought to clearly have a witness of truth in those days over 125 years ago. We thank thee for the manhood that is our heritage. Give us the guts and the gumption to teach it to our children, at our firesides, at our knees, in our homes, in our churches, and in our schools. Give us the guts and the gumption to stand up with respect before the battle flag and not to bow the knee for any reasons whatever. Give us love and kindness, but give us onto truth and justice. Now we thank thee for thy blessings as we continue the activities of this day. In Jesus name, Amen.

NOTES

1. Terry Rude, "Southern Manhood," Greenville, SC: 1991. Reprinted by permission of the speaker.
2. J. Steve Wilkins was an ordained minister in the Presbyterian Church in America (PCA) with a seminary degree from Reformed Theological Seminary in Jackson, Mississippi. He currently pastors the Church of the Redeemer in West Monroe, Louisiana which was forced out of the PCA in 2007 over Wilkins' white supremacist views. He co-authored a pamphlet with Douglas Wilson explaining their slavery apologia. Douglas Wilson and Steve Wilkins, *Southern Slavery: As It Was* (Moscow, ID: Canon Press, 1996).
3. Rude is citing the story from John William Jones, *Christ in the Camp; or, Religion in Lee's Army* (Richmond, Virginia: B. F. Johnson & Co, 1887), 404.

4. Robert G. Tanner, *Stonewall in the Valley* (New York: Doubleday, 1976) 153.
5. The Southern Baptist Theological Seminary was first located at the campus of Furman University in Greenville, South Carolina when it closed during the Civil War. It reopened in 1877 in Louisville, Kentucky.
6. Jones, *Christ in the Camp* 264.
7. Douglas Southhall Freeman, *Lee's Lieutenants: Manassas to Malvern Hill* (Ann Arbor: University of Michigan Press, 1942), XXVIII.
8. Geoffrey C. Ward, Ric Burns, and Ken Burns, *The Civil War: The Complete Text of the Bestselling Narrative History of the Civil War* (New York: Random House, 1990) 115.
9. Rude is citing the hagiographic biography of Bob Jones, Sr. written by Jones' employee Robert K. Johnson, *Builder of Bridges*. However, Bob Jones' father, Alex Jones was a member of the 37th Alabama Regiment and was *never* at Chickamauga. Rather he and the rest of the 37th were in Mississippi, where Alex Jones was captured at Vicksburg and allowed to return home. The 37th gathered again and Alex joined them since he received his pay on Lookout Mountain on October 31, 1863. One month before the 37th's Battle of Mill Creek Gap, however, Alex got an injury of his own on April 9, 1864—*not* at Chickamauga. The pension examiner three decades in the future would call the injury a "slight flesh wound below his right knee." He would receive CSA clothing on April 19, 1864, and was honorably discharged on April 26, 1865. Thirty years later, Alex himself is bragging to the *Ozark Banner-Advertiser* writers that he was at Chickamauga as part of Company H, 37th Alabama, proving that the fiction started with Alex. Robert K. Johnson, *Builder of Bridges: A Biography of Bob Jones, Sr.* (Greenville, South Carolina: Bob Jones University Press, 1969) 8. Thomas McAdory Owen, "Muster Roll of Captain Marion Searcy," *Report of the Alabama History Commission to the Governor of Alabama* (Montgomery, Alabama: Brown Printing, 1900) 346. *Compiled Service Records of Confederate Soldiers Who Served in Organizations from the State of Alabama* (Washington, D.C.: National Archives, 1862) 3. "William A. Jones," Alabama Civil War Service Database (Montgomery, Alabama: Alabama Department of Archives and History) https://archives. alabama.gov/civilwar/soldier.cfm?id= 107058. *Ozark Banner-Advertiser*, May 25, 1893, 3.
10. Noah W. Griffin, "Reunion in Black and White," *San Francisco Examiner*, March 13, 1991, 17.
11. John Brown Gordon, *Reminiscences of the Civil War* (New York: Charles Scribner), 445.

CHAPTER FOURTEEN

"The Right Side of History"

PHIL SNIDER

Springfield, Missouri
August 13, 2012[1]

In August 2012, the city of Springfield, Missouri considered adding sexual orientation to the city's non-discrimination ordinance. In a three-hour public hearing, more than sixty people talked, but Rev. Phil Snider, the pastor of Brentwood Christian Church, changed the whole conversation in a brief three-minute speech.[2] He quoted phrases from Southern white Protestant sermons—from white nationalist sermons—and simply changed their phrase "racial integration" to a more contemporary "gay rights." The audience was visibly squirming while he read his speech and jaws dropped when he finally revealed his strategy.

Snider's primary source was a fundamentalist quoted in this volume, Bob Jones, Sr. In Greenville, South Carolina, in 1960 and on Easter Sunday Morning—the highest holy day in Christianity—Bob Jones took to the radio to answer Billy Graham's "Good Friday" message that Southern white Protestants should embrace racial integration. Jones' reaction was his message "Is Segregation Scriptural?"[3] That is the predominant sermon which Snider counter-states in 2012. Americans have since judged Jones' ideology and religious practice to be out of step with our ideals of equality and justice.[4] How does Rev. Snider frustrate the religious prejudice against LGBTQ+ sexual identity in his counter-statement? In taking the words out of the mouths of white supremacists like Bob Jones and massaging them only slightly to match the current moment, how does Snider change his audience? How has our rhetoric remained similarly consistent over the last century? How can other sermons be analogously updated for contemporary issues?

After the city council voted 6–3 to pass this ordinance, the citizens of Springfield voted in 2015 to not use the more inclusive wording by a vote of 51.43% to 48.57%.[5]

Good evening. My name is the Rev. Dr. Phil Snider. I was born and raised in Springfield, Missouri, and I stand before you this evening in support of the ordinance.

I worry about the future of our city. Any accurate reading of the Bible should make it clear that gay rights go against the plain truth of the word of God. As one preacher warns us, man, in overstepping the boundary lines God has drawn by making special rights for gays and lesbians, has taken another step in the direction of inviting the Judgment of Almighty God upon our land. This step of gay rights is but another stepping stone toward the immorality and lawlessness that will be characteristic of the last days.[6]

This ordinance represents a denial of all that we believe in, and no one should force it on us. It's not that we don't care about homosexuals, but it said our rights would be taken away and unchristian views will be forced on us and our children for we'd be forced to go against our personal morals.[7]

Outside government agents are endeavoring to disturb God's established order. It is not in line with the Bible. Do not let people lead you astray.[8]

The liberals leading this movement do not believe the Bible any longer, but every good substantial, Bible-believing, intelligent, orthodox Christian can read the Word of God and know that what is happening is not of God.[9]

When you run into conflict with God's established order, you have trouble. You do not produce harmony. You produce destruction and trouble, and our city is in the greatest danger it has ever been in in its history. The reason is that we have gotten away from the Bible of our forefathers.[10]

You see, the right of segregation is clearly established by the Holy Scriptures, both by precept and example.[11]

One minute.

I'm sorry. I brought the wrong notes with me this evening. I borrowed my argument from the wrong century. It turns out what I've been reading to you are direct quotes from white preachers from times like the 1950s and 1960s, all in support of things like racial segregation. All I have done is taken out phrase, "racial integration," and substituted it with the phrase, "gay rights."

I guess the arguments I've been hearing around Springfield lately sounded so similar to these that I got them confused. I hope you won't make the same mistake. I hope you will stand on the right side of history.

Thank you.

NOTES

1. Phil Snider, "On Gay Rights," Springfield, Missouri, August 13, 2012. Reprinted by permission of the speaker.
2. Amos Bridges, "Springfield Pastor's Speech to Council Goes Viral," *Springfield News-Leader*, October 21, 2012, A1.
3. The story behind this sermon is available from Camille K. Lewis, "'Jim Crow Must Go!': Dueling Revivalists in Holy Week, 1960," Southeastern Commission for the Study of Religion, *American Academy of Religion*, Greenville, South Carolina. March 2013. The story behind the publication of this sermon text is available from Camille K. Lewis, "'A' is for Archive: The Politics of Research in the Southern Archive," *Carolina Communication Annual*, Vol. 31 (2015): 15–18. The sermon text itself is available at Bob Jones, "Is Segregation Scriptural?" April 15, 1960, Transcribed by Camille K. Lewis, https://www.drslewis.org/camille/2013/03/15/is-segregation-scriptural-by-bob-jones-sr-1960/.
4. The 1983 Supreme Court decision in *Bob Jones University v. The People of the United States* found that Bob Jones University's policies banning interracial dating are contrary to public policy because of the school's racial discrimination.
5. Dominic Holden, "Springfield, Missouri, Voters Repeal LGBT Rights Ordinance," *Buzzfeed News*, April 7, 2015.
6. After the 1954 *Brown v. Board* decision, Rev. James F. Burks of Norfolk, Virginia stated: "Rejecting the plain Truth of the Word of God has always resulted in the Judgment of God. Man, in overstepping the boundary lines God has drawn, has taken another step in the direction of inviting the Judgment of Almighty God. This step of racial integration is but another stepping stone toward the gross immorality and lawlessness that will be characteristic of the last days, just preceding the Return of the Lord Jesus Christ." As quoted in Jane Dailey, "The Theology of Massive Resistance: Sex, Segregation, and the Sacred after Brown," Ed. By Clive Webb, *Massive Resistance: Southern Opposition to the Second Reconstruction* (New York: Oxford University Press, 2005), 156.
7. Southern Baptist pastor, W. A. Criswell, at the South Carolina Baptist Evangelism Conference on February 22, 1956 labeled racial integration as something "forced" and "a denial of all that we believe in." Curtis W. Freeman, "'Never Had I Been So Blind': W. A. Criswell's 'Change' on Racial Segregation," *Journal of Southern Religion*, Vol 10, 2007, 1–12.
8. Jones stated in his 1960 radio address "When you run into conflict with God's established order racially, you have trouble. You do not produce harmony. You produce destruction and trouble, and this nation is in the greatest danger it has ever been in in its history. We are facing dangers from abroad and dangers at home, and the reason is that we have got away from the Bible of our forefathers. The best Christians who ever put foot on this earth since the Apostolic days were the men and women in America back in the old days. Some of them owned slaves, and some of them did not; and some of them were slaves, and some of them were not. Back in those days, they believed the Bible, and God called this nation into existence to be a witness to the world and to be true to the Word of God. Do not let these religious liberals blowing their bubbles of nothing over your head get you upset and disturbed. Let's get back to the Word of God and be sensible." Bob Jones, "Is Segregation Scriptural?"
9. Bob Jones, "Is Segregation Scriptural?"

10. Bob Jones, "Is Segregation Scriptural?"

11. Founder of Furman University and Southern Baptist minister, Richard Furman, wrote a letter to the Governor of South Carolina in 1838 that, in time, became public. He stated that "these sentiments, the Convention, on whose behalf I address your Excellency, cannot think just, or well-founded: for the right of holding slaves is clearly established by the Holy Scriptures, both by precept and example." Richard Furman, "The Views of Baptists, Relative to the Colored Population," Transcribed by T. Lloyd Benson, May 28, 1823, http://eweb.furman.edu/~benson / docs/rcd-fmn1.htm.

CHAPTER FIFTEEN

"Eulogy for State Senator and Pastor Clementa Pinckney"

BARACK OBAMA

Mother Emanuel A.M.E. Church, Charleston, South Carolina
June 25, 2015[1]

When a young white newcomer entered a Bible study at the Mother Emanuel Church in Charleston on June 17, 2015, the church members, in Christian charity, welcomed him and fed him. And shortly after, Dylann Roof killed those nine people of color while they prayed.

The white supremacist rhetoric produced by Council of Conservative Citizens had radicalized Dylann Roof and moved him to plan the massacre.[2] He intended to start a race war.[3] Instead his actions caused the Southern civic sphere to begin to question its memorials to slavery and its raising of battle flags. The Mother's Day before the massacre, Dylann Roof visited the Confederate Museum in Greenville, South Carolina where Terry Rude is president. Since Roof took pictures in front of the Museum and published them on social media, the connection could not be ignored. Rude spoke to the local media and, like in his "Southern Manhood" talk cited earlier in this volume, he asserted the bifurcated myth of the Old South. He said, Roof "represents something hellish, vicious, horrible, as base as could be base." Rude's museum, in contrast to Roof's crime, venerates all the beauty of South Carolina of "love [and] praying together."[4]

In this eulogy to State Senator and Pastor of Mother Emanuel Clementa Pinckney, President Barack Obama constructs a contrasting drama to Rude's. Rhetoricians consider this speech the finest of Obama's presidency. Obama praises Pinckney's character and life and highlights the unique community and history of the Black church.[5] For Obama, the Black church is outward-focused as opposed to Hargis and McIntire's belligerent inward-focus. What is the role of "grace" in Obama's rhetoric? Is it an agent, agency, or action? Are there counter-agents at work in this text? What is the attitude or incipient action? That is, what kind of action is Obama preparing America for in this talk?

Giving all praise and honor to God.

The Bible calls us to hope, to persevere, and have faith in things not seen.

"They were still living by faith when they died," Scripture tells us. "They did not receive the things promised; they only saw them and welcomed them from a distance, admitting that they were foreigners and strangers on Earth."

We are here today to remember a man of God who lived by faith. A man who believed in things not seen. A man who believed there were better days ahead, off in the distance. A man of service who persevered, knowing full well he would not receive all those things he was promised, because he believed his efforts would deliver a better life for those who followed.

To Jennifer, his beloved wife; to Eliana and Malana, his beautiful, wonderful daughters; to the Mother Emanuel family and the people of Charleston, the people of South Carolina.

I cannot claim to have the good fortune to know Reverend Pinckney well. But I did have the pleasure of knowing him and meeting him here in South Carolina, back when we were both a little bit younger. Back when I didn't have visible grey hair. The first thing I noticed was his graciousness, his smile, his reassuring baritone, his deceptive sense of humor—all qualities that helped him wear so effortlessly a heavy burden of expectation.

Friends of his remarked this week that when Clementa Pinckney entered a room, it was like the future arrived; that even from a young age, folks knew he was special—anointed. He was the progeny of a long line of the faithful—a family of preachers who spread God's word, a family of protesters who sowed change to expand voting rights and desegregate the South. Clem heard their instruction, and he did not forsake their teaching.

He was in the pulpit by 13, pastor by 18, public servant by 23. He did not exhibit any of the cockiness of youth, nor youth's insecurities; instead, he set an example worthy of his position, wise beyond his years, in his speech, in his conduct, in his love, faith, and purity.

As a senator, he represented a sprawling swath of the Lowcountry, a place that has long been one of the most neglected in America, a place still wracked by poverty and inadequate schools, a place where children can still go hungry and the sick can go without treatment, a place that needed somebody like Clem.

His position in the minority party meant the odds of winning more resources for his constituents were often long. His calls for greater equity were too often unheeded, the votes he cast were sometimes lonely. But he never gave up. He stayed true to his convictions. He would not grow discouraged. After a full day at the capitol, he'd climb into his car and head to the church to draw sustenance from his family, from his ministry, from the community that loved and needed him. There he would fortify his faith and imagine what might be.

Reverend Pinckney embodied a politics that was neither mean, nor small. He conducted himself quietly, and kindly, and diligently. He encouraged progress not by pushing his ideas alone, but by seeking out your ideas, partnering with you to make things happen. He was full of empathy and fellow feeling, able to walk in somebody else's shoes and see through their eyes. No wonder one of his senate colleagues remembered Senator Pinckney as "the most gentle of the 46 of us—the best of the 46 of us."

Clem was often asked why he chose to be a pastor and a public servant. But the person who asked probably didn't know the history of the AME church. As our brothers and sisters in the AME church know, we don't make those distinctions. "Our calling," Clem once said, "is not just within the walls of the congregation, but the life and community in which our congregation resides."

He embodied the idea that our Christian faith demands deeds and not just words, that the "sweet hour of prayer" actually lasts the whole week long, that to put our faith in action is more than individual salvation, it's about our collective salvation, that to feed the hungry and clothe the naked and house the homeless is not just a call for isolated charity but the imperative of a just society.

What a good man. Sometimes I think that's the best thing to hope for when you're eulogized—after all the words and recitations and resumes are read, to just say someone was a good man.

You don't have to be of high station to be a good man. Preacher by 13. Pastor by 18. Public servant by 23. What a life Clementa Pinckney lived. What an example he set. What a model for his faith. And then to lose him at 4—slain in his sanctuary with eight wonderful members of his flock, each at different stages in life but bound together by a common commitment to God.

Cynthia Hurd. Susie Jackson. Ethel Lance. DePayne Middleton-Doctor. Tywanza Sanders. Daniel L. Simmons. Sharonda Coleman-Singleton. Myra Thompson. Good people. Decent people. God-fearing people. People so full of life and so full of kindness. People who ran the race, who persevered. People of great faith.

To the families of the fallen, the nation shares in your grief. Our pain cuts that much deeper because it happened in a church. The church is and always has been the center of African-American life—a place to call our own in a too often hostile world, a sanctuary from so many hardships.

Over the course of centuries, Black churches served as "hush harbors" where slaves could worship in safety; praise houses where their free descendants could gather and shout hallelujah—rest stops for the weary along the Underground Railroad; bunkers for the foot soldiers of the Civil Rights Movement. They have been, and continue to be, community centers where we organize for jobs and justice; places of scholarship and network; places where children are loved and fed and kept out of harm's way, and told that they are beautiful and smart and taught that they matter. That's what happens in church.

That's what the Black church means. Our beating heart. The place where our dignity as a people is inviolate. When there's no better example of this tradition than Mother Emanuel—a church built by Blacks seeking liberty, burned to the ground because its founder sought to end slavery, only to rise up again, a Phoenix from these ashes.

When there were laws banning all-Black church gatherings, services happened here anyway, in defiance of unjust laws. When there was a righteous movement to dismantle Jim Crow, Dr. Martin Luther King, Jr. preached from its pulpit, and marches began from its steps. A sacred place, this church. Not just for Blacks, not just for Christians, but for every American who cares about the steady expansion of human rights and human dignity in this country; a foundation stone for liberty and justice for all. That's what the church meant.

We do not know whether the killer of Reverend Pinckney and eight others knew all of this history. But he surely sensed the meaning of his violent act. It was an act that drew on a long history of bombs and arson and shots fired at churches, not random, but as a means of control, a way to terrorize and oppress. An act that he imagined would incite fear and recrimination; violence and suspicion. An act that he presumed would deepen divisions that trace back to our nation's original sin.

Oh, but God works in mysterious ways. God has different ideas.

He didn't know he was being used by God. Blinded by hatred, the alleged killer could not see the grace surrounding Reverend Pinckney and that Bible study group—the light of love that shone as they opened the church doors and invited a stranger to join in their prayer circle. The alleged killer could have never anticipated the way the families of the fallen would respond when they saw him in court—in the midst of unspeakable grief, with words of forgiveness. He couldn't imagine that.

The alleged killer could not imagine how the city of Charleston, under the good and wise leadership of Mayor Riley, how the state of South Carolina, how the United States of America would respond—not merely with revulsion at his evil act, but with big-hearted generosity and, more importantly, with a thoughtful introspection and self-examination that we so rarely see in public life.

Blinded by hatred, he failed to comprehend what Reverend Pinckney so well understood—the power of God's grace.

This whole week, I've been reflecting on this idea of grace. The grace of the families who lost loved ones. The grace that Reverend Pinckney would preach about in his sermons. The grace described in one of my favorite hymnals—the one we all know:

> Amazing grace, how sweet the sound
> That saved a wretch like me.
> I once was lost, but now I'm found;
> Was blind but now I see.

According to the Christian tradition, grace is not earned. Grace is not merited. It's not something we deserve. Rather, grace is the free and benevolent favor of God as manifested in the salvation of sinners and the bestowal of blessings. Grace.

As a nation, out of this terrible tragedy, God has visited grace upon us, for he has allowed us to see where we've been blind. He has given us the chance, where we've been lost, to find our best selves. We may not have earned it, this grace, with our rancor and complacency, and short-sightedness and fear of each other—but we got it all the same. He gave it to us anyway. He's once more given us grace. But it is up to us now to make the most of it, to receive it with gratitude, and to prove ourselves worthy of this gift.

For too long, we were blind to the pain that the Confederate flag stirred in too many of our citizens. It's true, a flag did not cause these murders. But as people from all walks of life, Republicans and Democrats, now acknowledge—including Governor Haley, whose recent eloquence on the subject is worthy of praise—as we all have to acknowledge, the flag has always represented more than just ancestral pride. For many, Black and white, that flag was a reminder of systemic oppression and racial subjugation. We see that now.

Removing the flag from this state's capitol would not be an act of political correctness; it would not be an insult to the valor of Confederate soldiers. It would simply be an acknowledgment that the cause for which they fought—the cause of slavery—was wrong. The imposition of Jim Crow after the Civil War, the resistance to civil rights for all people was wrong. It would be one step in an honest accounting of America's history; a modest but meaningful balm for so many unhealed wounds. It would be an expression of the amazing changes that have transformed this state and this country for the better, because of the work of so many people of goodwill, people of all races striving to form a more perfect union. By taking down that flag, we express God's grace.

But I don't think God wants us to stop there. For too long, we've been blind to the way past injustices continue to shape the present. Perhaps we see that now. Perhaps this tragedy causes us to ask some tough questions about how we can permit so many of our children to languish in poverty, or attend dilapidated schools, or grow up without prospects for a job or for a career.

Perhaps it causes us to examine what we're doing to cause some of our children to hate. Perhaps it softens hearts towards those lost young men, tens and tens of thousands caught up in the criminal justice system and leads us to make sure that that system is not infected with bias; that we embrace changes in how we train and equip our police so that the bonds of trust between law enforcement and the communities they serve make us all safer and more secure.

Maybe we now realize the way racial bias can infect us even when we don't realize it, so that we're guarding against not just racial slurs, but we're also guarding against the subtle impulse to call Johnny back for a job interview but not Jamal. So that we search our hearts when we consider laws to make it harder for some of our fellow citizens to vote. By recognizing our common humanity by treating every child as important, regardless of the color of their skin or the station into which they were born, and to do what's necessary to make opportunity real for every American—by doing that, we express God's grace.

For too long—

AUDIENCE: For too long!

For too long, we've been blind to the unique mayhem that gun violence inflicts upon this nation. Sporadically, our eyes are open: When eight of our brothers and sisters are cut down in a church basement, twelve in a movie theater, 26 in an elementary school. But I hope we also see the thirty precious lives cut short by gun violence in this country every single day; the countless more whose lives are forever changed—the survivors crippled, the children traumatized and fearful every day as they walk to school, the husband who will never feel his wife's warm touch, the entire communities whose grief overflows every time they have to watch what happened to them happen to some other place.

The vast majority of Americans—the majority of gun owners—want to do something about this. We see that now. And I'm convinced that by acknowledging the pain and loss of others, even as we respect the traditions and ways of life that make up this beloved country—by making the moral choice to change, we express God's grace.

We don't earn grace. We're all sinners. We don't deserve it. But God gives it to us anyway. And we choose how to receive it. It's our decision how to honor it.

None of us can or should expect a transformation in race relations overnight. Every time something like this happens, somebody says we have to have a conversation about race. We talk a lot about race. There's no shortcut. And we don't need more talk. None of us should believe that a handful of gun safety measures will prevent every tragedy. It will not. People of goodwill will continue to debate the merits of various policies, as our democracy requires. This is a big, raucous place, America is. And there are good people on both sides of these debates. Whatever solutions we find will necessarily be incomplete.

But it would be a betrayal of everything Reverend Pinckney stood for, I believe, if we allowed ourselves to slip into a comfortable silence again. Once the eulogies have been delivered, once the TV cameras move on, to go back to business as usual—that's what we so often do to avoid uncomfortable truths about the prejudice that still infects our society. To settle for symbolic gestures without following up with the hard work of more lasting change—that's how we lose our way again.

It would be a refutation of the forgiveness expressed by those families if we merely slipped into old habits, whereby those who disagree with us are not merely wrong but bad; where we shout instead of listen; where we barricade ourselves behind preconceived notions or well-practiced cynicism.

Reverend Pinckney once said, "Across the South, we have a deep appreciation of history. We haven't always had a deep appreciation of each other's history." What is true in the South is true for America. Clem understood that justice grows out of recognition of ourselves in each other. That my liberty depends on you being free, too. That history can't be a sword to justify injustice, or a shield against progress, but must be a manual for how to avoid repeating the mistakes of the past—how to break the cycle. A roadway toward a better world. He knew that the path of grace involves an open mind—but, more importantly, an open heart.

That's what I've felt this week—an open heart. That, more than any particular policy or analysis, is what's called upon right now, I think what a friend of mine, the writer Marilyn Robinson, calls "that reservoir of goodness, beyond, and of another kind, that we are able to do each other in the ordinary cause of things."

That reservoir of goodness. If we can find that grace, anything is possible. If we can tap that grace, everything can change.

> Amazing grace. Amazing grace.
> Amazing grace, how sweet the sound,
> That saved a wretch like me;
> I once was lost, but now I'm found;
> Was blind but now I see.

Clementa Pinckney found that grace.
Cynthia Hurd found that grace.
Susie Jackson found that grace.
Ethel Lance found that grace.
DePayne Middleton-Doctor found that grace.
Tywanza Sanders found that grace.
Daniel L. Simmons, Sr. found that grace.
Sharonda Coleman-Singleton found that grace.
Myra Thompson found that grace.

Through the example of their lives, they've now passed it on to us. May we find ourselves worthy of that precious and extraordinary gift, as long as our lives endure. May grace now lead them home. May God continue to shed His grace on the United States of America.

NOTES

1. Barack Obama, "Eulogy for State Senator and Pastor Clementa Pinckney," Charleston, SC, June 26, 2015, https://obamawhitehouse.archives.gov/the-press-office/2015/06/26/remarks-president-eulogy-honorable-reverend-clementa-pinckney.

2. Southern Poverty Law Center, "The Council of Conservative Citizens: Dylann Roof's Gateway into the World of White Nationalism," *Southern Poverty Law Center*, June 20, 2015, https://www.splcenter.org/hatewatch/2015/06/21/council-conservative-citizens-dylann-roofs-gateway-world-white-nationalism.

3. Ralph Ellis, Greg Botelho, Ed Payne, "Charleston church shooter hears victim's kin say, 'I forgive you,'" *CNN.com*, June 1, 2015, https://www.cnn.com/2015/06/19/us/charleston-church-shooting-main/.

4. Myra Ruiz, "Confederate Museum and Library Official Calls Dylann Roof 'Evil,'" *WYFF*, June 23, 2015, http://www.wyff4.com/article/ confederate-museum-and-library-official-calls-dylann-roof-evil/7015447.

5. For a thorough analysis of Obama's eulogy see David A. Frank, "The Act of Forgiveness in Barack Obama's Eulogy for the Honorable Reverend Clementa Pinckney, Charleston, SC, June 26, 2015," *Rhetoric, Race, Religion, and the Charleston Shootings: Was Blind But Now I See* (Lexington, Kentucky: Lexington Books 2019).

CHAPTER SIXTEEN

"On Removing Confederate Statues"

MITCH LANDRIEU

New Orleans
May 18, 2017[1]

Nearly two years after Dylann Roof's massacre, the city of New Orleans removed three statues to the Confederacy: Robert E. Lee (erected in 1884), P. G. T. Beauregard (erected in 1913), and Jefferson Davis (erected in 1911). Hiring a contractor to remove the statues was difficult since local firms received harassment and death threats. An out-of-state firm finally agreed to do the job, but its workers wore bullet-proof vests and masks to protect themselves and their identities.[2] After their removal, Mayor Mitch Landrieu delivered this speech. The New Yorker *said the speech "challenged the flawed morality" of the Lost Cause.[3]* Esquire *called it "an honest account of history," relieved that someone was finally stating the obvious: "Landrieu systematically eviscerates all the non-history by which the Confederate States of America were repurposed as a device to justify Jim Crow and white supremacy. Landrieu's indictment gave immunity to nobody for the crimes against history these monuments represented."[4]*

At his alma mater, The Catholic University of America, *Landrieu explained in 2018 that his faith was foundational to his political belief that all people deserve fair treatment. When he was in the Louisiana state legislature at the same time as KKK wizard David Duke, Landrieu realized that the South had never really dealt with its white supremacy: "That incident really seared me for a long time .... There needs to be a reconciliation, and we can't do that without a recognition that what happened before was a terrible, terrible mistake. Slavery is this nation's original sin."[5]*

In his 2017 speech, Landrieu's faith is not overt but is undergirding its rhetoric. How does his faith come through his words? How does he counter-state the nostalgia of the Lost Cause? Whom does he cite as his moral allies in the justification for removing the statues? How does he address his adversaries?

The soul of our beloved City is deeply rooted in a history that has evolved over thousands of years; rooted in a diverse people who have been here together every step of the way—for both good and for ill.

It is a history that holds in its heart the stories of Native Americans: the Choctaw, Houma Nation, the Chitimacha. Of Hernando de Soto, Robert Cavelier, Sieur de La Salle, the Acadians, the Islenos, the enslaved people from Senegambia, Free People of Color, the Haitians, the Germans, both the empires of France and Spain. The Italians, the Irish, the Cubans, the South and Central Americans, the Vietnamese and so many more.

You see, New Orleans is truly a city of many nations, a melting pot, a bubbling cauldron of many cultures.

There is no other place quite like it in the world that so eloquently exemplifies the uniquely American motto: *e pluribus unum*—out of many we are one.

But there are also other truths about our city that we must confront. New Orleans was America's largest slave market: a port where hundreds of thousands of souls were brought, sold and shipped up the Mississippi River to lives of forced labor of misery of rape, of torture.

America was the place where nearly 4,000 of our fellow citizens were lynched, 540 alone in Louisiana; where the courts enshrined 'separate but equal'; where Freedom Riders coming to New Orleans were beaten to a bloody pulp.

So when people say to me that the monuments in question are history, well, what I just described is real history as well, and it is the searing truth.

And it immediately begs the questions: why there are no slave ship monuments, no prominent markers on public land to remember the lynchings or the slave blocks; nothing to remember this long chapter of our lives; the pain, the sacrifice, the shame—all of it happening on the soil of New Orleans?

So for those self-appointed defenders of history and the monuments, they are eerily silent on what amounts to this historical malfeasance, a lie by omission.

There is a difference between remembrance of history and reverence of it. For America and New Orleans, it has been a long, winding road, marked by great tragedy and great triumph. But we cannot be afraid of our truth.

As President George W. Bush said at the dedication ceremony for the National Museum of African American History & Culture, "A great nation does not hide its history. It faces its flaws and corrects them."

So today I want to speak about why we chose to remove these four monuments to the Lost Cause of the Confederacy, but also how and why this process can move us towards healing and understanding of each other.

So, let's start with the facts.

The historic record is clear: the Robert E. Lee, Jefferson Davis, and P.G.T. Beauregard statues were not erected just to honor these men, but as part of the movement which became known as The Cult of the Lost Cause. This 'cult' had one goal—through monuments and through other means—to rewrite history to hide the truth, which is that the Confederacy was on the wrong side of humanity.

First erected over 166 years after the founding of our city and 19 years after the end of the Civil War, the monuments that we took down were meant to rebrand the history of our city and the ideals of a defeated Confederacy.

It is self-evident that these men did not fight for the United States of America. They fought against it. They may have been warriors, but in this cause they were not patriots.

These statues are not just stone and metal. They are not just innocent remembrances of a benign history. These monuments purposefully celebrate a fictional, sanitized Confederacy; ignoring the death, ignoring the enslavement, and the terror that it actually stood for.

After the Civil War, these statues were a part of that terrorism as much as a burning cross on someone's lawn; they were erected purposefully to send a strong message to all who walked in their shadows about who was still in charge in this city.

Should you have further doubt about the true goals of the Confederacy, in the very weeks before the war broke out, the Vice President of the Confederacy, Alexander Stephens, made it clear that the Confederate cause was about maintaining slavery and white supremacy.

He said in his now famous "Cornerstone Speech" that the Confederacy's "cornerstone rests upon the great truth, that the negro is not equal to the white man; that slavery—subordination to the superior race—is his natural and normal condition. This, our new government, is the first, in the history of the world, based upon this great physical, philosophical, and moral truth."[6]

Now, with these shocking words still ringing in your ears, I want to try to gently peel from your hands the grip on a false narrative of our history that I think weakens us and make straight a wrong turn we made many years ago so we can more closely connect with integrity to the founding principles of our nation and forge a clearer and straighter path toward a better city and more perfect union.

Last year, President Barack Obama echoed these sentiments about the need to contextualize and remember all of our history. He recalled a piece of stone, a slave auction block engraved with a marker commemorating a single moment in 1830 when Andrew Jackson and Henry Clay stood and spoke from it.

President Obama said, "Consider what this artifact tells us about history ... on a stone where day after day for years, men and women ... bound and bought and sold and bid like cattle on a stone worn down by the tragedy of over a thousand bare feet. For a long time the only thing we considered important, the singular thing we once chose to commemorate as history with a plaque were the unmemorable speeches of two powerful men."[7]

A piece of stone—one stone. Both stories were history. One story told. One story forgotten or maybe even purposefully ignored.

As clear as it is for me today, for a long time, even though I grew up in one of New Orleans' most diverse neighborhoods, even with my family's long proud history of fighting for civil rights, I must have passed by those monuments a million times without giving them a second thought.

So I am not judging anybody. I am not judging people. We all take our own journey on race. I just hope people listen like I did when my dear friend Wynton Marsalis helped me see the truth. He asked me to think about all the people who have left New Orleans because of our exclusionary attitudes.

Another friend asked me to consider these four monuments from the perspective of an African American mother or father trying to explain to their fifth-grade daughter who Robert E. Lee is and why he stands atop of our beautiful city. Can you do it?

Can you look into that young girl's eyes and convince her that Robert E. Lee is there to encourage her? Do you think she will feel inspired and hopeful by that story? Do these monuments help her see a future with limitless potential? Have you ever thought that if her potential is limited, yours and mine are too?

We all know the answer to these very simple questions.

When you look into this child's eyes is the moment when the searing truth comes into focus for us. This is the moment when we know what is right and what we must do. We can't walk away from this truth.

And I knew that taking down the monuments was going to be tough, but you elected me to do the right thing, not the easy thing, and this is what that looks like. So relocating these Confederate monuments is not about taking something away from someone else. This is not about politics. This is not about blame or retaliation. This is not a naïve quest to solve all our problems at once.

This is, however, about showing the whole world that we as a city and as a people are able to acknowledge, understand, reconcile and, most importantly, choose a better future for ourselves, making straight what has been crooked and making right what was wrong.

Otherwise, we will continue to pay a price with discord, with division, and yes, with violence.

To literally put the Confederacy on a pedestal in our most prominent places of honor is an inaccurate recitation of our full past. It is an affront to our present, and it is a bad prescription for our future.

History cannot be changed. It cannot be moved like a statue. What is done is done. The Civil War is over. And the Confederacy lost, and we are better for it.

Surely we are far enough removed from this dark time to acknowledge that the cause of the Confederacy was wrong.

And in the second decade of the twenty-first century, asking African Americans—or anyone else—to drive by property that they own; occupied by reverential statues of men who fought to destroy the country and deny that person's humanity seems perverse and absurd.

Centuries-old wounds are still raw because they never healed right in the first place.

Here is the essential truth: we are better together than we are apart. Indivisibility is our essence. Isn't this the gift that the people of New Orleans have given to the world?

We radiate beauty and grace in our food, in our music, in our architecture, in our joy of life, in our celebration of death; in everything that we do. We gave the world this funky thing called jazz; the most uniquely American art form that is developed across the ages from different cultures.

Think about second lines, think about Mardi Gras, think about muffaletta, think about the Saints, gumbo, red beans and rice. By God, just *think*. All we hold dear is created by throwing everything in the pot; creating, producing something better; everything a product of our historic diversity.

We are proof that out of many we are one—and better for it! Out of many, we are one—and we really do love it!

And yet, we still seem to find so many excuses for not doing the right thing. Again, remember President Bush's words, "A great nation does not hide its history. It faces its flaws and corrects them."

We forget, we deny how much we really depend on each other, how much we need each other. We justify our silence and inaction by manufacturing noble causes that marinate in historical denial. We still find a way to say "wait, not so fast."

But like Dr. Martin Luther King Jr. said, "wait has almost always meant never."

We can't wait any longer. We need to change. And we need to change now. No more waiting. This is not just about statues, this is about our attitudes and behavior as well. If we take these statues down and don't change to become a more open and inclusive society this would have all been in vain.

While some have driven by these monuments every day and either revered their beauty or failed to see them at all, many of our neighbors and fellow Americans see them very clearly. Many are painfully aware of the long shadows their presence casts, not only literally but figuratively. And they clearly receive the message that the Confederacy and the cult of the lost cause intended to deliver.

Earlier this week, as the cult of the Lost Cause statue of P.G.T Beauregard came down, world renowned musician Terence Blanchard stood watch, his wife Robin and their two beautiful daughters at their side.

Terence went to a high school on the edge of City Park named after one of America's greatest heroes and patriots, John F. Kennedy. But to get there he had to pass by this monument to a man who fought to deny him his humanity.

He said, "I've never looked at them as a source of pride. It's always made me feel as if they were put there by people who don't respect us. This is something I never thought I'd see in my lifetime. It's a sign that the world is changing."

Yes, Terence, it is, and it is long overdue.

Now is the time to send a new message to the next generation of New Orleanians who can follow in Terence and Robin's remarkable footsteps.

A message about the future, about the next 300 years and beyond; let us not miss this opportunity New Orleans and let us help the rest of the country do the same. Because now is the time for choosing. Now is the time to actually make this the City we always should have been, had we gotten it right in the first place.

We should stop for a moment and ask ourselves—at this point in our history, after Katrina, after Rita, after Ike, after Gustav, after the national recession, after the BP oil catastrophe and after the tornado—if presented with the opportunity to build monuments that told our story or to curate these particular spaces—would these monuments be what we want the world to see? Is this really our story?

We have not erased history. We are becoming part of the city's history by righting the wrong image these monuments represent and crafting a better, more complete future for all our children and for future generations.

And unlike when these Confederate monuments were first erected as symbols of white supremacy, we now have a chance to create not only new symbols, but to do it together, as one people.

In our blessed land we all come to the table of democracy as equals.

We have to reaffirm our commitment to a future where each citizen is guaranteed the uniquely American gifts of life, liberty and the pursuit of happiness.

That is what really makes America great and today it is more important than ever to hold fast to these values and together say a self-evident truth that out of many we are one. That is why today we reclaim these spaces for the United States of America.

Because we are one nation, not two; indivisible with liberty and justice for all, not some. We all are part of one nation, all pledging allegiance to one flag, the flag of the United States of America. And New Orleanians are in, all of the way.

It is in this union and in this truth that real patriotism is rooted and flourishes.

Instead of revering a 4-year brief historical aberration that was called the Confederacy we can celebrate all 300 years of our rich, diverse history as a place named New Orleans and set the tone for the next 300 years.

After decades of public debate, of anger, of anxiety, of anticipation, of humiliation and of frustration. After public hearings and approvals from three separate community led commissions. After two robust public hearings and a 6–1 vote by the duly elected New Orleans City Council. After review by 13 different federal and state judges. The full weight of the legislative, executive, and judicial branches of government has been brought to bear and the monuments in accordance with the law have been removed.

So now is the time to come together and heal and focus on our larger task. Not only building new symbols, but making this city a beautiful manifestation of what is possible and what we as a people can become.

Let us remember what the once exiled, imprisoned and now universally loved Nelson Mandela and what he said after the fall of apartheid. "If the pain has often been unbearable and the revelations shocking to all of us, it is because they indeed bring us the beginnings of a common understanding of what happened and a steady restoration of the nation's humanity."[8]

So before we part let us again state the truth clearly.

The Confederacy was on the wrong side of history and humanity. It sought to tear apart our nation and subjugate our fellow Americans to slavery. This is the history we should never forget and one that we should never again put on a pedestal to be revered.

As a community, we must recognize the significance of removing New Orleans' Confederate monuments. It is our acknowledgment that now is the time to take stock of, and then move past, a painful part of our history. Anything less would render generations of courageous struggle and soul-searching a truly lost cause.

Anything less would fall short of the immortal words of our greatest President Abraham Lincoln, who with an open heart and clarity of purpose calls on us today to unite as one people when he said: "With malice toward none, with charity for all, with firmness in the right as God gives us to see the right, let us strive on to finish the work we are in, to bind up the nation's wounds, to do all which may achieve and cherish: a just and lasting peace among ourselves and with all nations."[9]

Thank you.

NOTES

1. Mitch Landrieu, "On Removing Confederate Monuments," New Orleans, 2017. Reprinted by permission of the speaker.
2. "New Orleans takes down White Supremacist Monument," *Daily Review* (Morgan City, Louisiana), April 25, 2017, 3. Bill Turque, "Confederate Statue Moved from Rockville Courthouse over the Weekend," *Washington Post*, July 24, 2017.
3. Jelani Cobb, "Bill Maher, Mitch Landrieu, and Echoes of the Civil War," *The New Yorker*, June 15, 2017. https://www.newyorker.com/news/daily-comment/bill-maher-mitch-landrieu-and-echoes-of-the-civil-war.

4. Charles P. Pierce, "This is What an Honest Account of History Looks Like," *Esquire*, May 23, 2017. https://www.esquire.com/news-politics/politics/news/a55221/landrieu-new-orleans-confederate-monuments/.

5. "Mitch Landrieu to Community: 'Diversity is Our Strength,'" November 19, 2018, https://communications.catholic.edu/news/2018/11/mitch-landrieu-talk.html.

6. Alexander H. Stephens, "Cornerstone Speech," March 21, 1861.

7. Barack Obama, "Remarks by the President at the Dedication of the National Museum of African American History and Culture," September 24, 2016, https://obamawhitehouse.archives.gov/the-press-office/2016/09/24/remarks-president-dedication-national-museum-african-american-history.

8. Nelson Mandela, "Receiving the Report of the TRC, October 29, 1998," *In His Own Words* (New York: Little, Brown, 2018).

9. Abraham Lincoln, "Second Inaugural Address," March 4, 1865.

Confessing the Sin of White Nationalism

CHAPTER SEVENTEEN

"Ending Racial Segregation in the Church"

JAMES WILLIAMS

2Cities Church, Montgomery, Alabama
August 4, 2019[1]

From Reconstruction through Civil Rights, from Revivalism through contested Confederate Memory, America has long wrestled with its Original Sin of white rule. How we talked in 1900 has not changed too much in 120 years, but as Burke underlines, the necessary counter-statements have always been present in our statements. We can find ways to be persistently heterodox within the white nationalist orthodoxy. When we are in Rome, we can do as the Greeks!

This last text demonstrates that resistance. In August 2019, Pastor James Williams was feeling the heaviness of Montgomery's long-standing white supremacist rule. Williams is part of the African American Ministries in the Presbyterian Church in America, and his 2Cities church is confronting the civic and ecclesiastical double consciousness within Alabama's Capital City. The same city in which white supremacist evangelist Bob Jones, Sr. got his public start—debuting his sermon "Modern Woman" in 1911 just four blocks West of 2Cities Church—is now the city in which Williams ministers as a seminary-trained, African American pastor in a Southern-born Presbyterian denomination. Williams himself is a living counter-statement.

On this August Sunday morning, several Bob Jones University graduates listen, sitting with their white and Black brothers and sisters, trying to learn how to repent of the white nationalist ideology they inherited. Williams started his sermon playing a clip from PBS's American Experience *episode about Alabama's most vocal segregationist governor, George Wallace, called "Setting the Woods on Fire." The selection begins with Wallace's son describing his father's "own suffering and the purification that brings and the enlightenment that brings, and his realization that some things he had done and said could have caused others to suffer bothered him and concerned him as a Christian." The video continues to explain that Wallace called the people he had used "as punching bags" over the years "and asked for their forgiveness."*

One person Wallace phoned was civil rights leader and U. S. Representative from Georgia, John Lewis—James Forman's former SNCC colleague—who remembers that Wallace "literally poured out his soul and heart to me. It was almost like a confession, like I was his priest. He was telling me everything that he did, some things that were wrong and that he was not proud of."

After playing that video clip, Pastor Williams begins. He starts in conversation with a white supremacist Governor who, in his own twilight, counter-stated his life and ideology. Dramatistically, Williams' attitude is a racially integrated church. How does he cast the actors in his drama? Compare Williams' actors to Rude's and to Jones'. How do their actions differ? How does Williams demonstrate that unified future in his rhetoric?

George Wallace gave a speech where he said, "segregation now, segregation tomorrow, segregation forevermore." And yet, at the end of his life, God called him to a great repentance that brought healing to a lot of people. I submit that to you, because some would tell us that it's just sort of a pipe dream that churches could come together, Black and white, because we worship different. You guys sing quiet and soft, and we sing loud and shouting, "AMEN!" But I submit to you, there's a higher calling. There's a God who's called us to be something, to represent a kingdom, the invisible kingdom, the kingdom that's coming. We are citizens of heaven, and we are to bring that citizenship to bear on earth while we are here.

When people encounter the body of Christ, they need to encounter the kingdom of God in reality. The kingdom of God for eternity is the kingdom for all people: for every tribe, for every nation, for every nationality. It is the gospel to preach it to every nation. So, we have sinned as a church. We have bought into the lie of segregation. This morning, I want to try to establish for us a theology of desegregation. Because segregation is very akin to racism. It is the byproduct of racism. It perpetuates the idea that racism is okay. And the last place that needs to be upheld is the church. So, I want to say to us, God wants to end segregation in the church. God wants to end racism in the church. Judgment begins with the household of God. We can't tell the world to not be racist. We can't tell the world, "You need to be this," "You need to be that," if we haven't dealt with our own stuff.

What I love about this group is … these folks are saying, "I was racist, I was raised racist, my family was racist." And they thought I'd frown and be all weirded out, and they said "I got convicted. It hadn't been that long ago—2012—and I wanted to change and I wanted to do something different." That was bringing hope to me. That's bringing help to me. That's exciting to me. I had to deal with my own stuff. We've all been touched by race, and God has called us as his people, as his ambassadors, as his representatives, to proclaim the Good News. God so loved the world, the entire world, that he gave his only begotten Son—the only way of salvation. There is no other name under Heaven where by men must be saved. [We should] proclaim that in life, words, and deeds, and action and love of Christ.

Racism defined, the dictionary says, as "prejudice, prejudging, discrimination, antagonism directed against someone of a different race based on belief that one's own race is superior." [It] goes on to say, "racism appears to be a word of recent origin with no citations currently known that would suggest the word was in use prior to the early 20th century." But the fact that the word is fairly new does not prove that the concept of racism does not exist in the distant past. There would be some who say, "This is a new word. We don't really need to talk about race because it's a new word." But language is just part of our history …. Long before people saw a spaceship they used to talk about spaceships. So, just because it wasn't used years ago, there were people enslaving people, the Scots were hating the British.…

In case you didn't know, I love you guys, you of the lighter hue. I call you my light-skin brothers and sisters. To the Black community, you have dark-skin and brown-skin, and you have light-skin. We are all in the same family, so you all are my light-skin brothers. You have ethnicity, believe it or not. It's white ethnicity, and it's a good thing. And I have ethnicity, and it's African and it's Black, and it's beautiful. And coming together in the name of Christ, in the name of the Gospel, has to be a powerful thing that will transform this world. Don't you want to be a part of that? …

God said we should be one. On the day of Pentecost … they "came together," and "each heard them in their own language" speaking the word of God.[2] And the Church began. So now in this book of Ephesians, Paul is addressing both groups, Jews and Gentiles. …

Now, this seems kind of complicated so I'm going to theologian Charles Hodge to kind of explain this. He gives a good explanation. Charles Hodge explains that in the Old Testament, God lived in the Temple. Those living near his dwelling place, having access to him, were his people. Israel was near …. The Gentiles were far away, and they were referred to as far away …. They lived at a distance and had no freedom of access to the place where God revealed his presence. And among the later Jews, the acts of receiving proselytes, people who were non-Jews becoming Jews, were called "making them near." Being far from God included both separation from his people, spiritual distance, and alienation from God himself. So Hodge concludes to be near includes both introduction to two things: introduction to the Church and reconciliation to God. These two ideas are clearly present and intended by the Apostle in the whole context that this double reconciliation is affected through the blood of Christ.[3]

So it's this idea that now that you have come to faith in Christ. It doesn't matter what our nationality was or the fact that we were considered a people near to God. You are now near to God too. You were brought near by the blood of Christ. By the cross of Jesus, you are as acceptable and as near as a people as we are. So, thus I say to you, the cross of Christ ends racism. The cross brings complete end to separations and any hostilities based on ethnic differences. In other words, the cross ends any form of racism or segregation.

So my suggestion today is: God wants an end to segregation in his church. I'm going to give you three things from the text. I believe this is straight from the theology that is here. Theology is the study of God, his character, who he is, his ways and what he expects. And we can look in these verses and see what he thinks about this whole issue of race and coming together. Three things: the cross ends racial segregation, the cross ends racial hostility, the cross ends racial superiority ....

I told this story last night, and my wife and I discovered it. When I met her, she told me about her uncle Vernon Dahmer. You can look him up, but turns out he's quite a historic figure in civil rights. They have a memorial made to him, and he's with all the martyrs of civil rights killed by the Klan. He was killed in 1966 on January 10th by the Klan because he was signing people to vote. He was in Hattiesburg, Mississippi. He had his own business. He was successful, but he was signing people up. He signing people up like Medgar Evers and helped establish SNCC .... He was getting death threats, so he was sleeping in cycles. And one night, the Klan shows up, and they throw gas bombs into his house, set his house on fire. He's waking up with shotgun blasts coming through the window. Imagine that—a successful businessman who got jobs for Black and white folks who had his own businesses. And now he's faced with this. So he grabbed the shotgun that he kept nearby the bed, and was holding them off so that he could get his little girl out the back window.... And Uncle Vernon Dahmer survived, and he managed to get out and get to the hospital. But he had been burned from the waist up, and his lungs had smoke inhalation, and he died that night. But his last words were "You don't vote, you don't matter." Those were his dying words. So he's a hero in the faith.

And when I got here [to Montgomery] I was standing by his memorial, and it was as if God was talking to me through him ... I was so afraid to come here.... "I don't know if I can come here, Lord. I don't know if I can do it. I don't know if I can pastor a church full of white folk in Montgomery." Can I be honest?...

And it was as if he said to me, "so you're scared, huh? What do you think I was? Why do you think I died? ... I died so that Black people can have opportunity."

Integration has changed education. It's changed government. It's changed society. Don't you think it's time for desegregation of the church?... God has called us to his kingdom work, and it's *his* church and [we are] to represent his church as his church should be represented. Any form of segregation, any form of racism in the church is a mockery of the cross. It shames the gospel. It's not God's intent.

Let's get into what God says in his Word ....We don't separate anymore. We have a bigger calling. He says to us today, we can no longer separate based on any cultural excuses we may offer.

Interracial dating—I was told by some of the elders of a very notable church—interracial marriages is the bottom line why we don't want to have a joint service and an interracial church. I said, "That's so sad because how can you say I don't need you when we're all in the same body of Christ. The hand can't say to the foot, 'I don't need you.'"...

If we repent like George Wallace did, I think there might be some hope for you and me. We may have had problems in the past, we may have a disgusting history that we are ashamed to talk about, we may be embarrassed about it, but that was at one time. "All things have become new." We are new creations in Christ.[4]...

Racism could be considered a thing of lust if you check out some of these people. They're craving hatred and indulging in the desires of the flesh and of the mind. I know it's a fleshly activity. It's not from God's spirit, and we are by nature children of wrath even as the rest....

It is a mysterious thing that a poor Black boy who is the son of a sharecropper is in Montgomery, Alabama and is pastoring a church that is mostly white. Oh my God, what a mystery according to his purpose which he set forth .... Desegregation of the church is long overdue, but it's a long haul and an uphill climb. Don't you fool yourself about the opposers, the haters, the naysayers, the doubters, and the theologians who are going to have their versions to justify as Miriam tried to justify with Moses, "What you doing married to that Ethiopian?" You see what God thought about it; she broke out with leprosy.[5] God didn't play around with this. Never has.

The cross ends this idea of separation, division for any reason in Christ. .... Segregation is at the core of it. To have any other attitude or to do anything different is to make a mockery of the cross. To insist on a segregated church is completely hostile to God's plan and intentions for his creation. What are we going to be doing a thousand years from now? Worshiping together, praising together, enjoying the Lord together .... God is pouring out his spirit, his grace on all people groups, and we should not be polarized because we're Black or because we're white. And anything obstinate to coming together is against God's will. God wants to end segregation in the church....

Not only does the cross end racial segregation and racial hostility, the cross ends racial superiority .... That's why Paul says, "so then you also are no longer strangers and aliens, but you are fellow citizens with the Saints and members of the House of God."[6] There is no superiority. God has declared us all the same by making us part of his household built on the foundation of the apostles and the prophets and Christ Jesus himself and said, "You are equal. You are welcome. There is dignity in every person."... People can't see the reality of God's Spirit if we're covered in our foggy views of what race dynamics are, and our flesh is in the way of allowing God's Spirit to make us a beautiful church that he's calling us to be ....

We are ambassadors of Christ. He has given us the ministry of reconciliation .... Ask God to show you what he would have you do. Open the gospel to every tribe and every nation because God wants to end segregation in the church.

NOTES

1. James Williams, "Ending Racial Segregation in the Church," Montgomery, AL, August 4, 2019. Reprinted by permission of the speaker.
2. Acts 2: 6–8.
3. Charles Hodge, *Systematic Theology, Volume 1* (Grand Rapids, MI: Christian Classics Ethereal Library, 2005) 399.
4. 2 Corinthians 5:17.
5. Numbers 12.
6. Ephesians 2:19.

Speaking of Religion

Daniel S. Brown, *Series Editor*

Speaking of Religion grows from a scholarly attentiveness to the role that religion plays in the public sphere. The decline of religious thought in public affairs is a common yet false narrative in the United States. Americans remain a devout people who are motivated to action by their faith commitments. Several contemporary, interdisciplinary scholars including Jürgen Habermas, Charles Taylor and Tariq Ramadan point us toward the privilege that religion and faith enjoys in public life. Collectively their work asserts that the world has entered a post-secular era: Secularism is dead and faith is alive. Speaking of Religion features short books, no more than 60,000 words or approximately 150 pages in length.

For additional information about this series or for the submission of manuscripts, please contact:

Erika Hendrix, Acquisitions Editor
e.hendrix@peterlang.com

To order books, please contact our Customer Service Department:

peterlang@presswarehouse.com (within the U.S.)
order@peterlang.com (outside the U.S.)

Or browse online by series at www.peterlang.com